HOW TO DRAW THE CAT

By MABEL L. GREER

WITH AN INTRODUCTION BY

FRANK M. RINES

COACHWHIP PUBLICATIONS

Greenville, Ohio

How to Draw the Cat, by Mabel L. Greer
Copyright © 2013 Coachwhip Publications
No claims made on public domain material.
First published 1940.
Front cover: Cat © Vitaliy Pakhnyushchyy

ISBN 1-61646-189-6
ISBN-13 978-1-61646-189-8

CoachwhipBooks.com

INTRODUCTION

For many years Miss Greer has been observing and studying cats, as well as drawing and painting them. Needless to say she loves cats else she never would have devoted so much of her time to the task.

After a long and pleasurable acquaintance with her models, and after receiving a definite thrill at viewing each new sketch or portrait of one of them, I suggested that some of these drawings be published in book form.

With the hope that they will give to you the same pleasure that the artist herself has experienced, they are herewith presented. Unlike many people whose hobby is pets and who specialize in some one breed, Miss Greer has among her feline friends representatives of almost every breed. These include nearly every color as well. In her text Miss Greer has mentioned the importance of a constant study of the cat in all its different attitudes and actions. This cannot be emphasized too strongly. Merely attempting to draw what one sees is not enough. A thorough understanding of whatever subject one may be drawing is an absolute necessity.

To the art student and to the artist who wishes either to learn how to draw cats, or having already done so, to increase his skill, I can most emphatically recommend a careful study of both pictures and text.

To the lover of cats, and there are legions of us, all of the sketches will be very interesting, and many will wish to detach and frame some of the full page drawings.

FRANK M. RINES.

Table of Contents and List of Illustrations

	PAGE
CATS TO LOVE AND TO DRAW	6
TOPAZE	7
A CIRCLE	9
HEADS	10
TEXTURE	12
FOUR SLEEPY CATS—IOLANTHE	13
SUGGESTIVE LINES AND SOLIDS	14
PICCOLO	15
EYES	16
DEMONSTRATING EARS	17
HEADS AND CIRCLES	18
NOSE AND MOUTH	19
NOSE AND MOUTH	20
CIRCLES AND OVALS	21
CAUTION	22
DORÉ	23
PAWS	24
FEATHERY PAWS	25
DARK AND LIGHT COMPOSITION—DOUBLE PAWS	26
PADS AND PAWS	27
ELMO	28
CHILLA—AMBER	29
THE TWINS AT PLAY—TOPAZE	30
MORNING SUN—I CAN CATCH YOU	31
YOUNG TOPAZE	32
CHARM AND PERSONALITIES	33
A LINE OF DORÉ—THE PROTECTOR ASLEEP	34
SKETCHES OF WHITE CATS	35
A BONNY BASKET	36
THE QUEEN—I MUST HAVE CLEAN FEET	37
BRIGHT LIGHT ON WHITE	38
FULL MEASURE	39
A HAIR OUT OF PLACE	40
CURVES AND CONTORTIONS—A COMFORTING PILLOW	41
EXPRESSIVE LINES—LABOR OF LOVE	42
SATIN AND DOWN	43
GROUP	44
DID YOU SPEAK—SIESTA	45
ATTITUDES	46
CUDDLY POSES	47
LINES OF RHYTHM	48
SUGGESTIONS	49
HEADS	50
THUMBS UP—HEAD	51
PRIMPING—HEAD	52
SLEEP	53
DORÉ	54
CONTENTMENT	55
IOLANTHE SLEEPS AGAINST GOLD	56
SKELETON	57

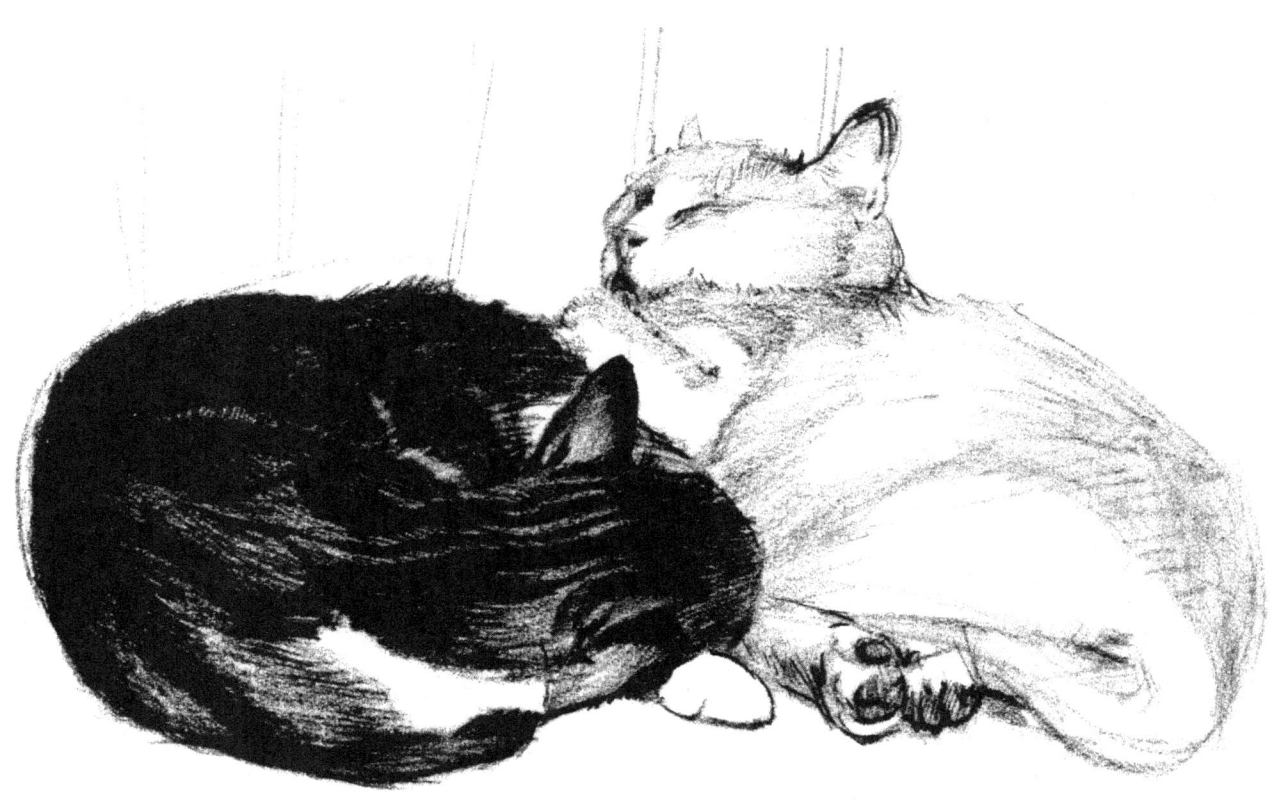

CATS TO LOVE AND TO DRAW

Come into my book and meet the nicest cats; not all thorobreds, but one hundred per cent fine cats, homey, lovable, independent and gorgeous, yet dependent on you for kindness and protection. You have cats yourself and you will find them all over the world ready at the faintest flicker of an eye to give unlimited affection, charm and amusement.

The attention called to the close study of the cat will be an enlightenment to those who just love cats as well as to those who wish to draw them.

When unexpectedly you meet a curled up bunch of fur like Amber and Patricia Blue-Eye above or a figure of gold in the sunlight like Topaze opposite, so appealing and breath taking, that you must drop everything to make a hasty record of it before it is lost forever, then is the time you will appreciate having your paper and pencil within reach. Always keep it around the house, the studio and yourself to do the cats and kittens when, where and as you find them. You will have to do just that as the cats are models that do not pose for you and even when asleep are continually moving. It demands rapid work and quick thinking on your part, at times acrobatic, for often you have to stand or again you have to sit on the floor.

There may be only a few seconds for an action line, a few minutes' study for form where circles and ovals will make a short cut to build on quickly. See to it the paper is large enough that you can make a new sketch with every change of the cats' position or part of the cat. Forget the eraser in this rough work.

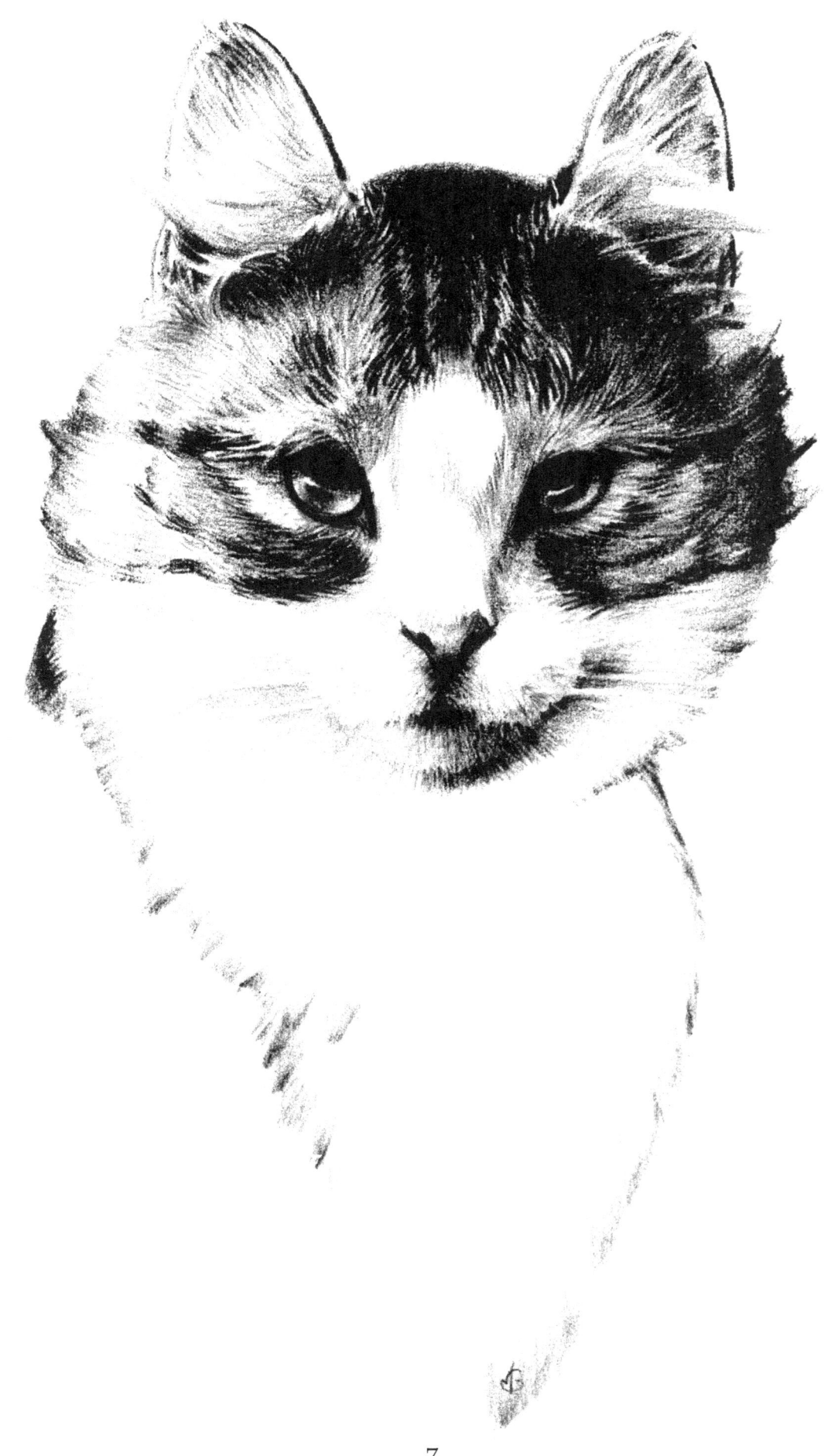

Make as many lines as are needed to get your impressions, keep those for future reference, making a new rendering for your finished drawing.

By placing a thin piece of paper over your sketch you can see the outline sufficiently to eliminate unnecessary lines and make a clean drawing for your finished study.

Lithograph crayons in pencil form with very sharp points were used for the sketches in this book, number four and number one, using number four to lay in, gradually working to number one for the rich dark tones. This pencil gives a very fine technique for cat fur.

Water color is an excellent, spontaneous medium when working for hues.

Oil paint thinned with your favorite medium to the same consistency of water-color makes a good, speedy foundation to build on. When making a finished drawing be very careful not to lose the life and lightness of your first sketch.

When your model is restless make notations of parts, as paws, legs, ears, eyes, shoulders, hips, tail, nose and mouth. Study them carefully, sketch them in all positions and at all angles. Study the growth and texture of the fur, the direction of each hair as it follows the form like flowing water in a brook.

Markings are distinctions in themselves, are most important and help immensely in establishing a recognizable portrait or sketch. When observing the markings you will be amazed at the beauty and rhythm of the design and the varied patterns. They are distinctions that when spoken of bring a mental picture of the animal in question, like the tabi, mackerel stripe, tiger stripe, calico, tortoise and plain color.

The construction of the skeleton is quite like the human skeleton only on all four paws, and the muscles are the same.

There is nothing mysterious about a cat. True there are times when you catch the steady straight-forward, straight-through-you look of its eye that you wonder how many million years it has known, what it thinks. Topaze in the sketch has that look.

Concentrated study of the cat with a pencil or minutes to hours of just plain observation is recreational as well as educational.

Store the study notes away in your mental library to be drawn on at will. They pay big dividends.

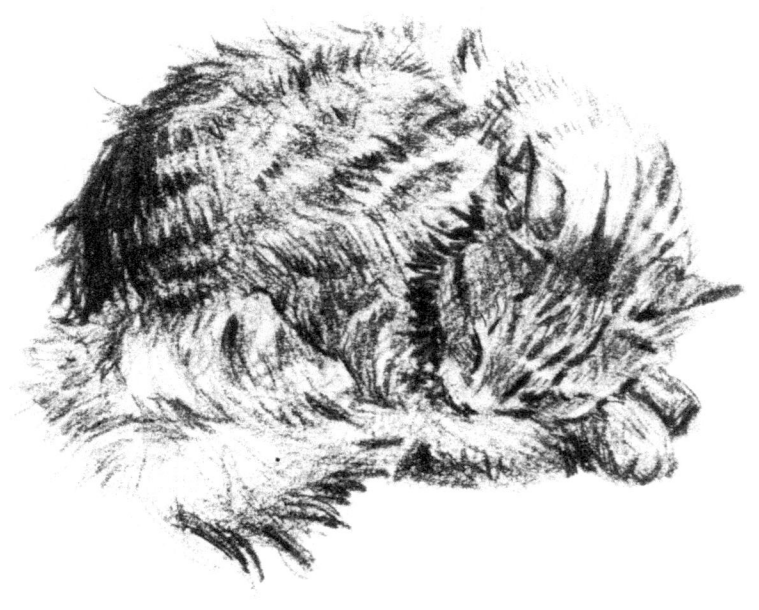

A CIRCLE

The sketch shows what take place in a circle and how circles play an important part to quickly establish the parts as well as the whole.

Doré asleep with the light streaming on her is an interesting subject for color as well as texture. Doré's coloring is the soft browns of the puma with the seal brown tabi markings and rather longish fur. She has an unusual tail, curled at the end with long fur giving the appearance of the bob cat, a woodsy looking bundle of fur that makes you reach for a pencil to capture her likeness before she moves.

Notice the markings are intense in the half light, becoming lost in the shimmer of high light as it hits the gloss of fur and again is lost in the dark of the shadow.

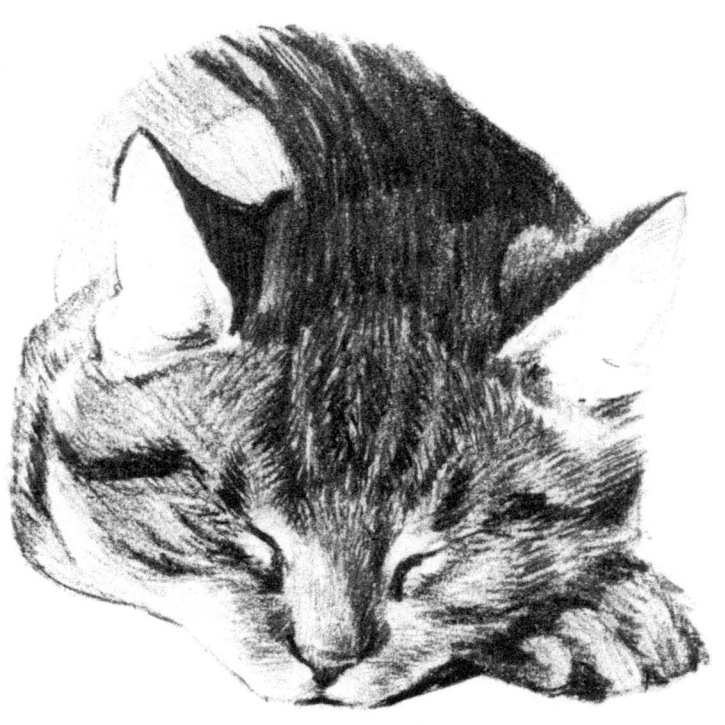

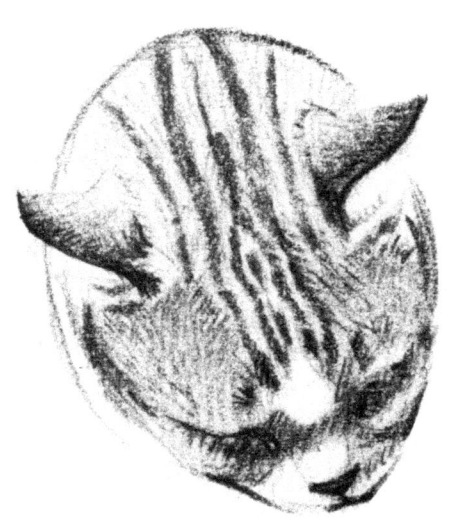

These heads show construction, texture and markings; while the skull is oval, the fur gives an appearance of roundness, therefore, a circle divided into four parts, one half for the top and forehead to eyes, divide distance from eyes to bottom of circle for nose, again divide distance from end of nose to bottom of circle for mouth, divide top of head one-half of placement of the front of ears.

Kittens, like babies, have a large head and full forehead.

There is a great fascination of sketching the head and studying the character of the features in all positions and under varied lightings.

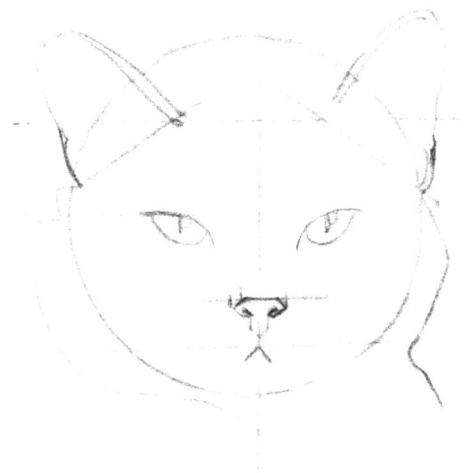

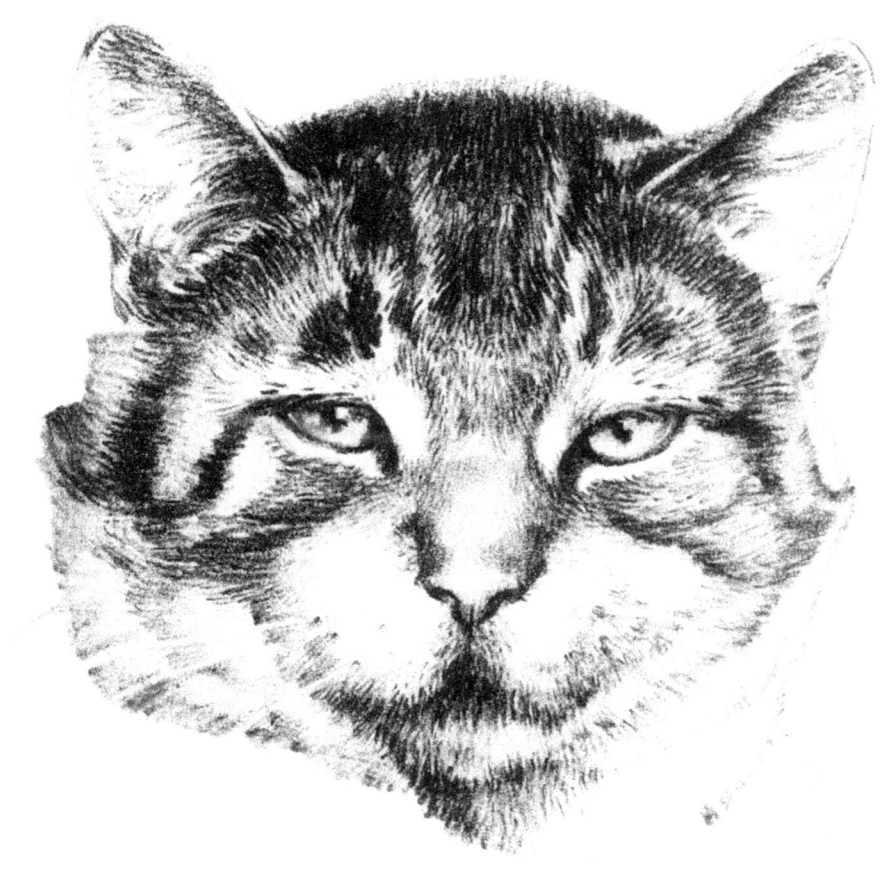

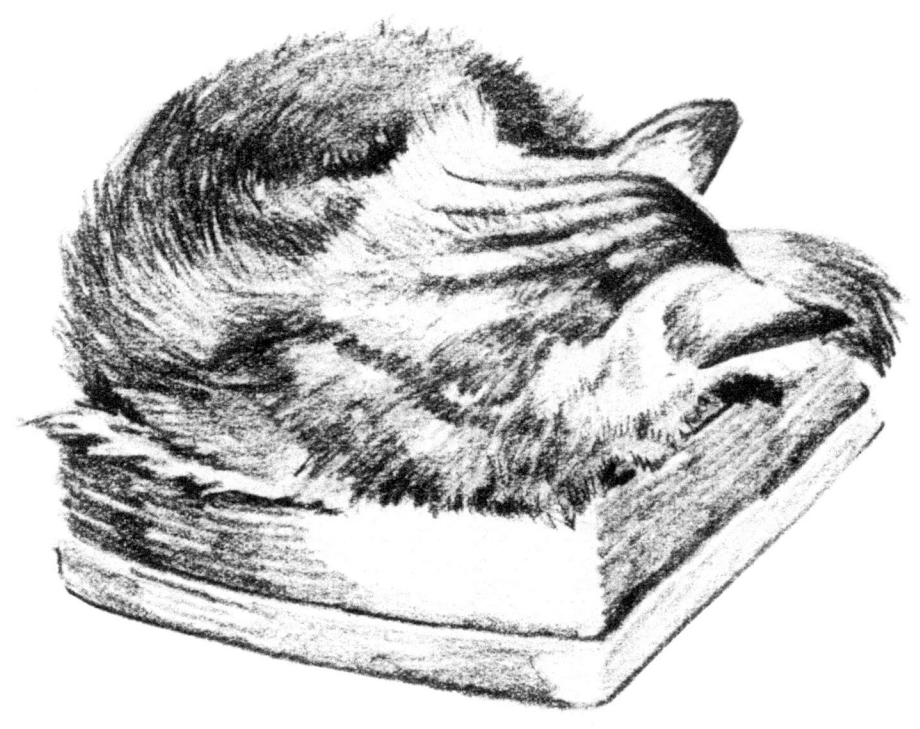

TEXTURE

All cats love boxes and baskets, the smaller the box, the more they have to squeeze into them the better they like it, and when there are several cats the one that gets possession of the box first is going to stay there for an unlimited time without much change, allowing you your best chance to bring a sketch somewhere near completion on the spot.

In the winter especially I keep baskets and boxes of all shapes and sizes near the heat and in the sun to lure the cats into them and give me the opportunity to get some interesting drawings.

Two or three, even one in a box is most amusing; you will notice in this pile of cats the beautiful lines flowing into each other and the contrast of curves with the straight lines of the box or basket.

The sketch above shows the lovely sweep of line from head to tip of the tail showing beyond the ears.

The four sleepy cats were a problem in speed, placing them on the paper rapidly, working on one to somewhere near a finish suggesting texture and markings, hurrying to do the next and the next until all were drawn. This was a wonderful opportunity to study all parts of the body, the head and all detail, the line of forearms and paw, the curve of the body and tail and the refreshing relaxation of the whole cat.

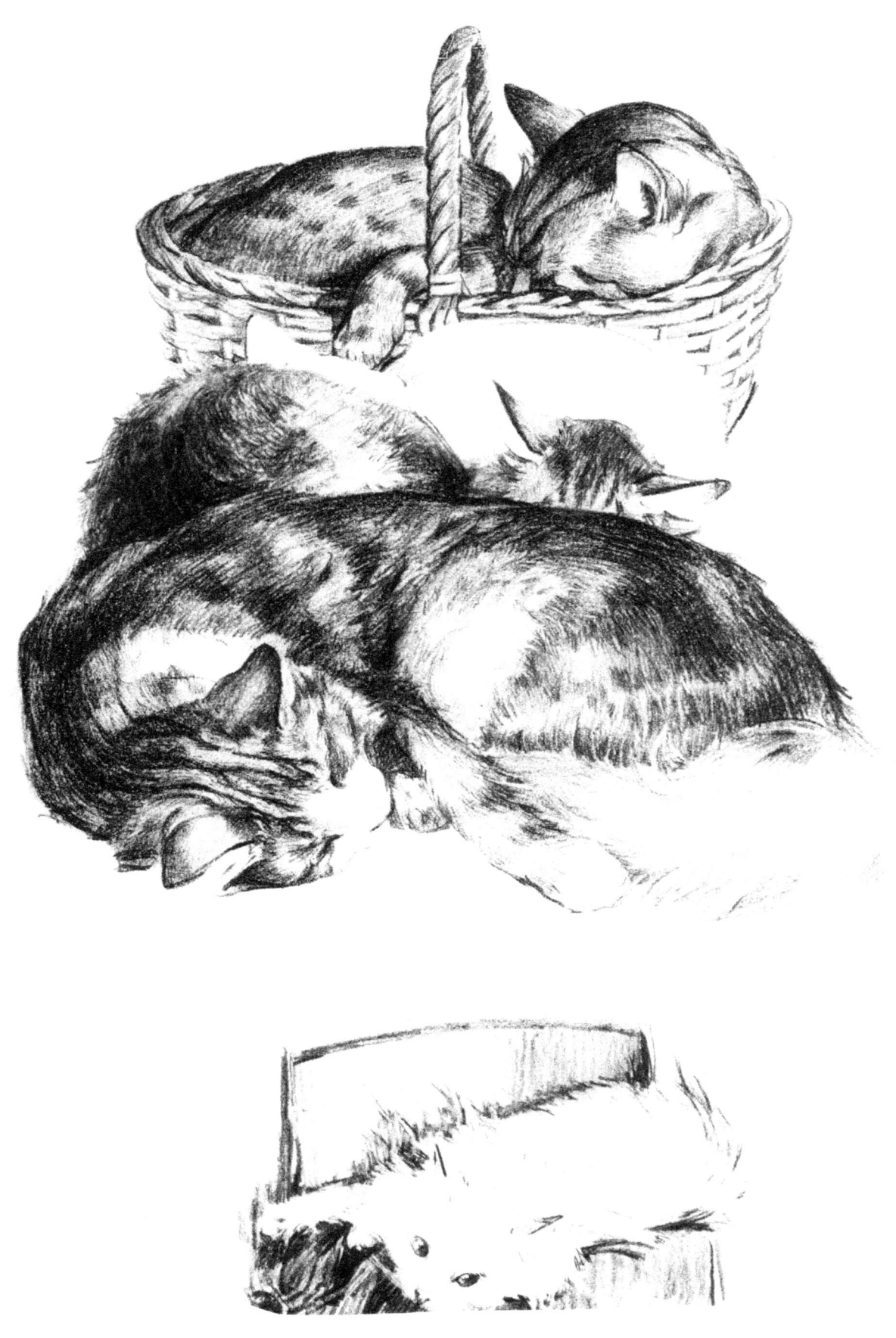

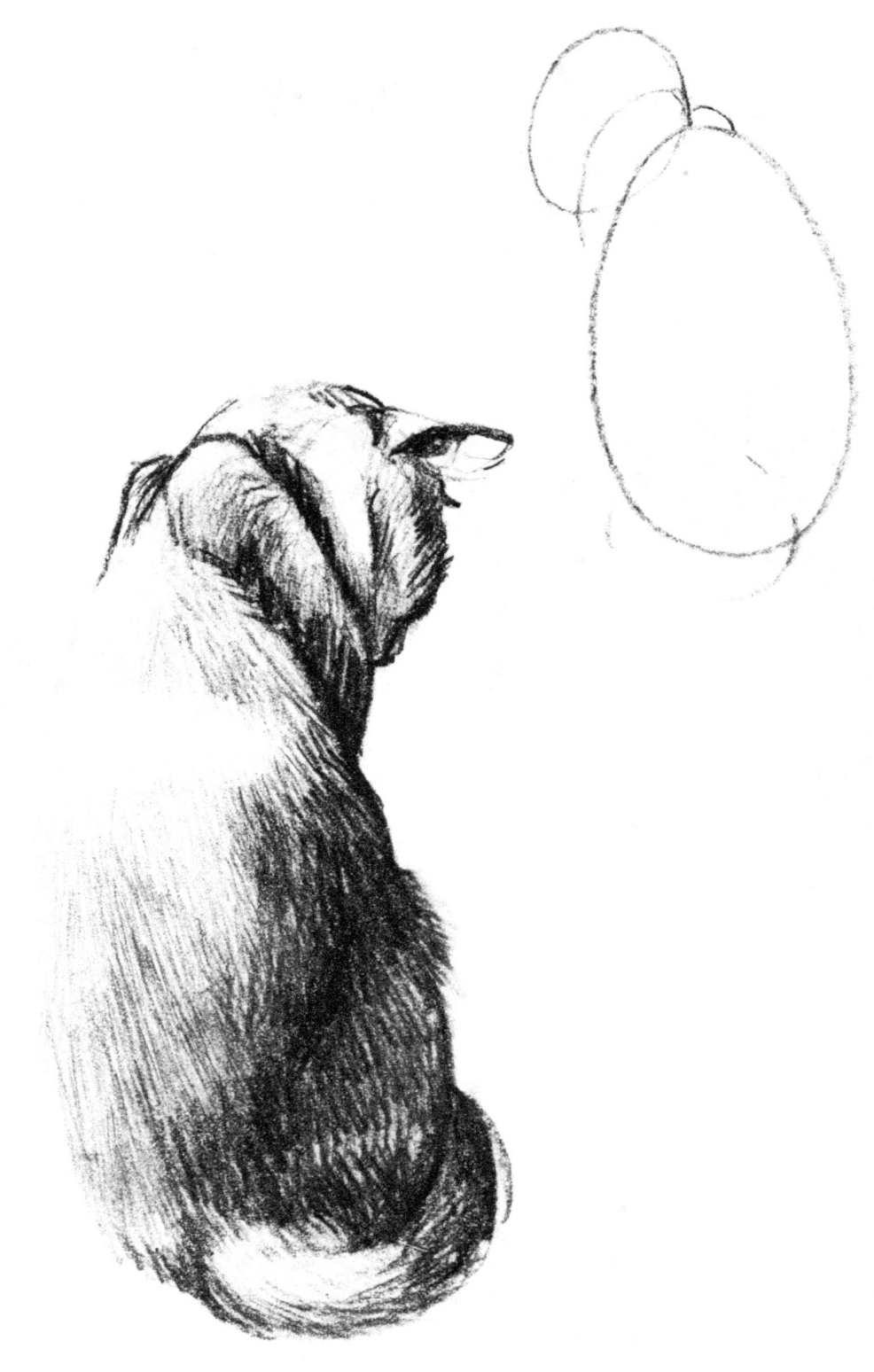

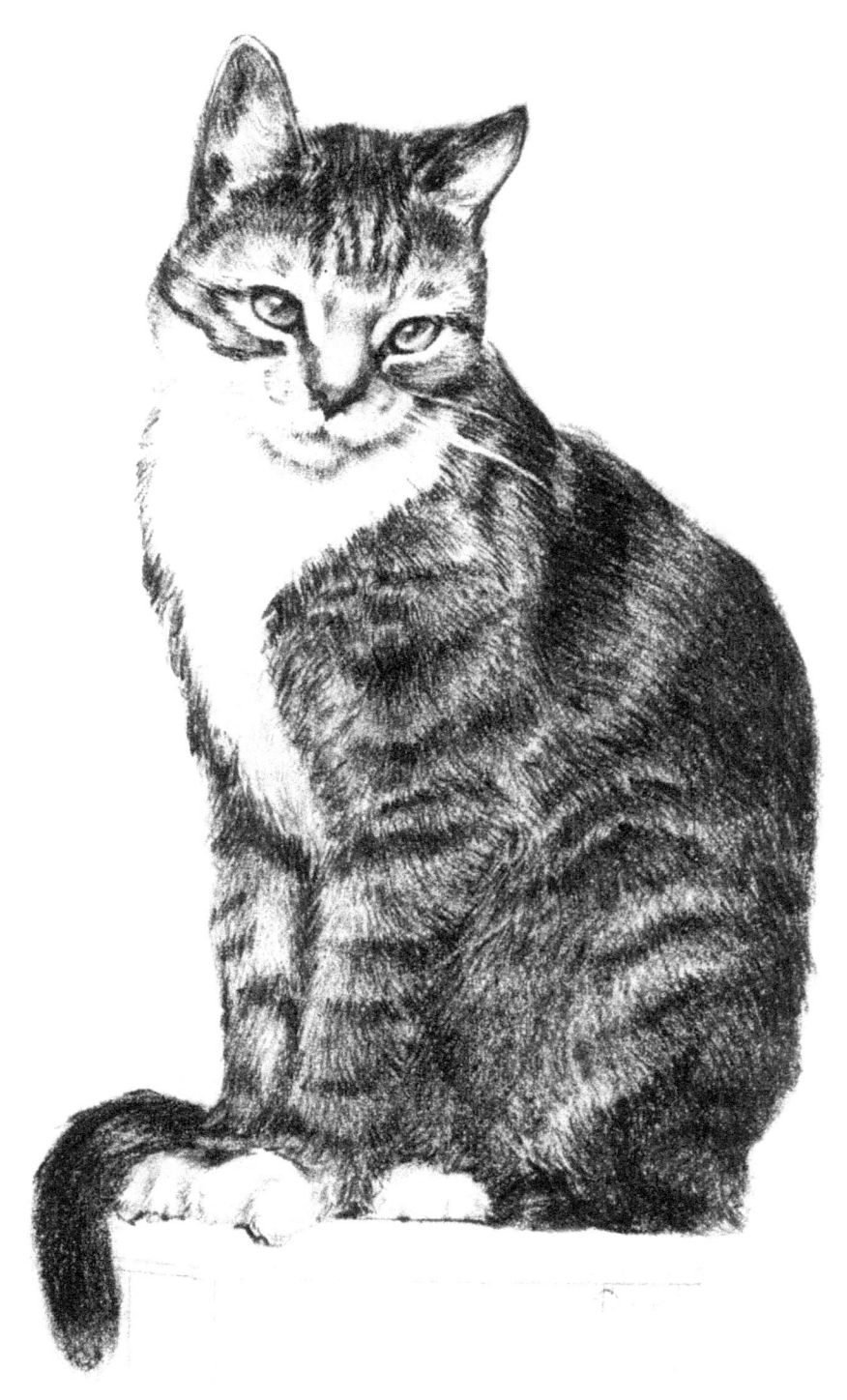

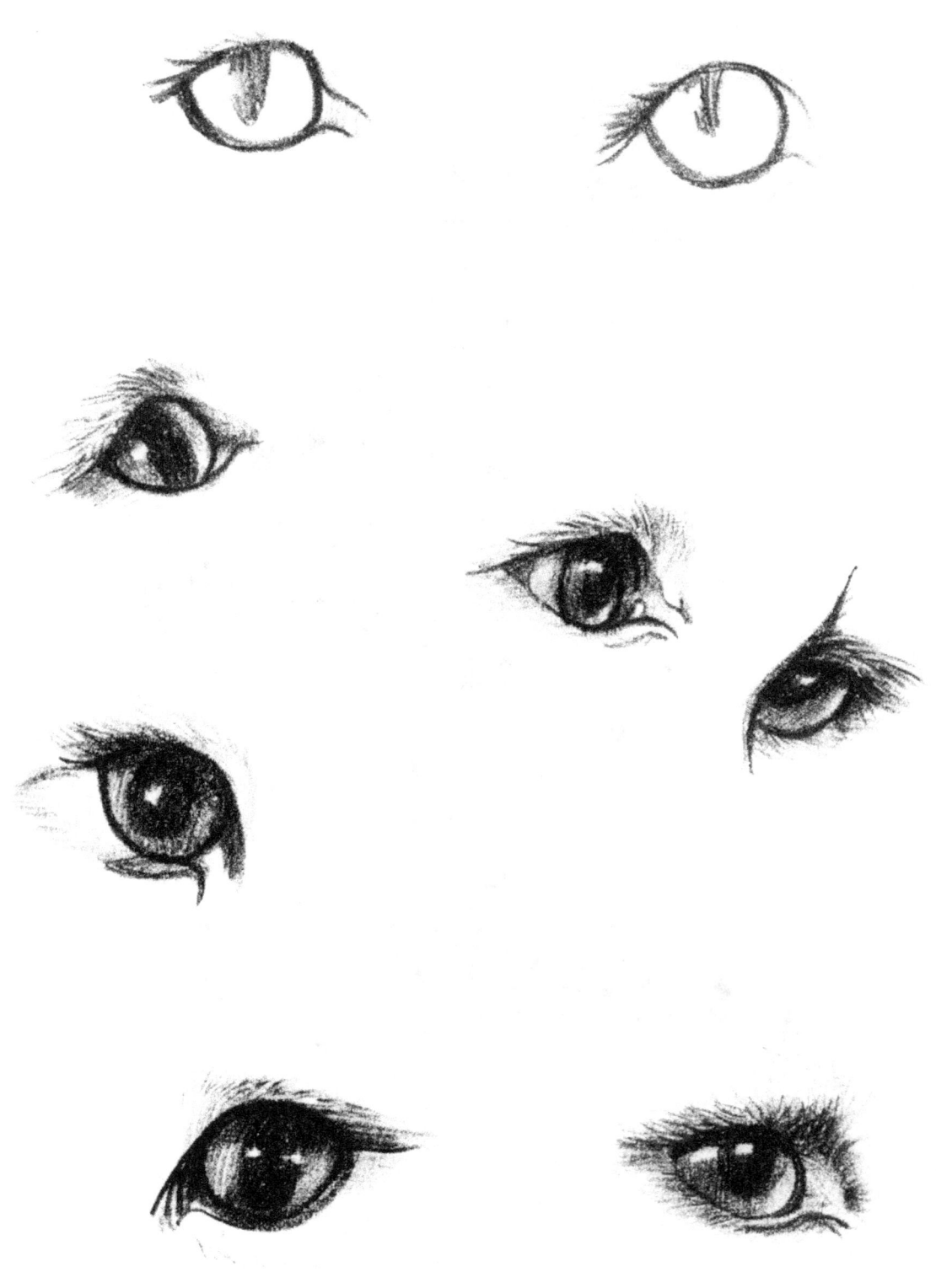

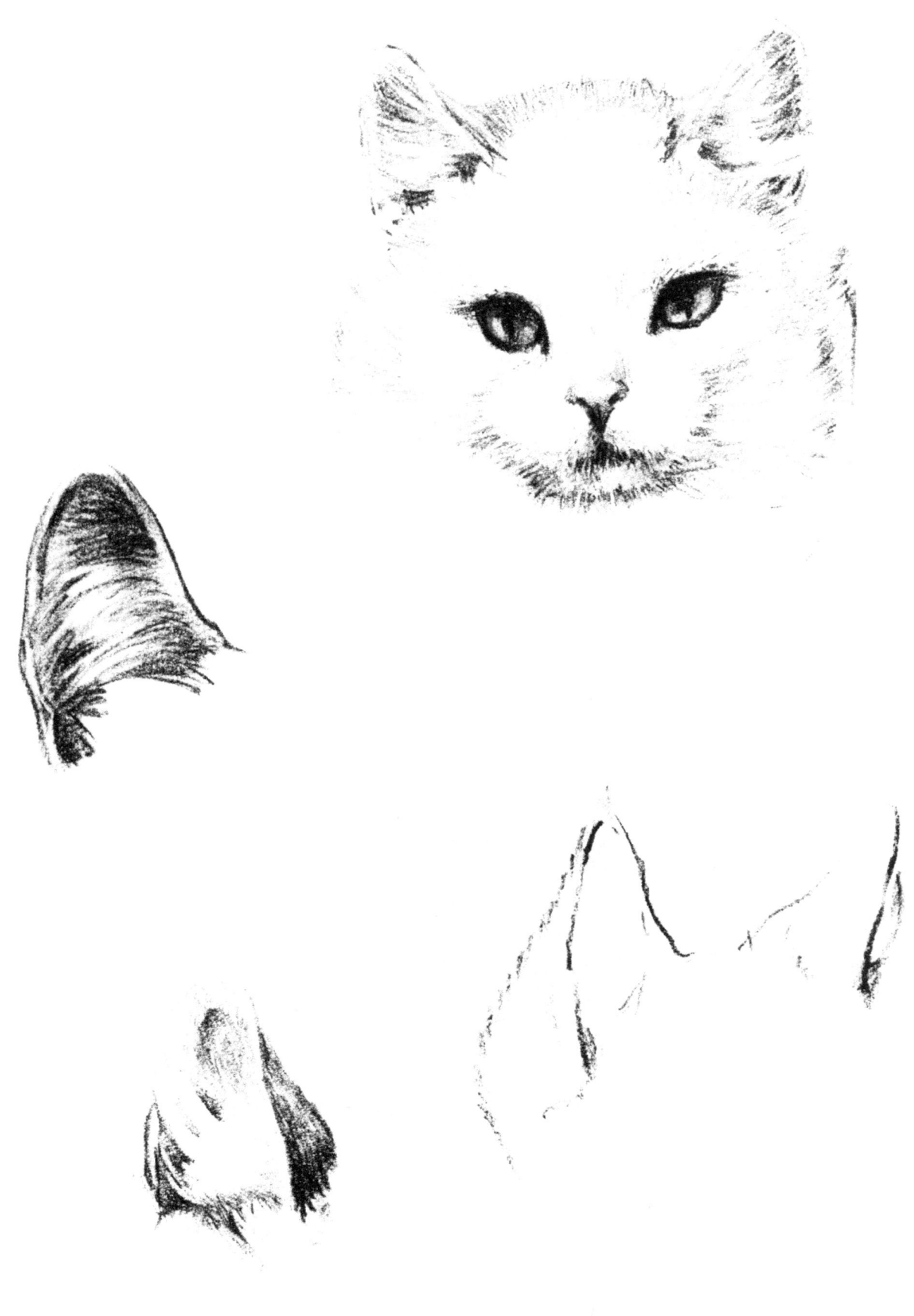

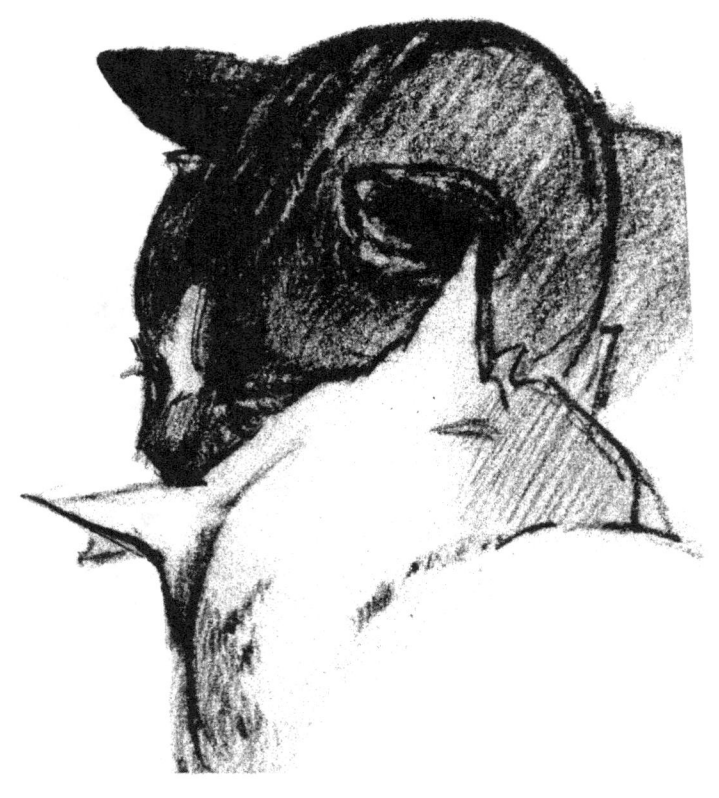

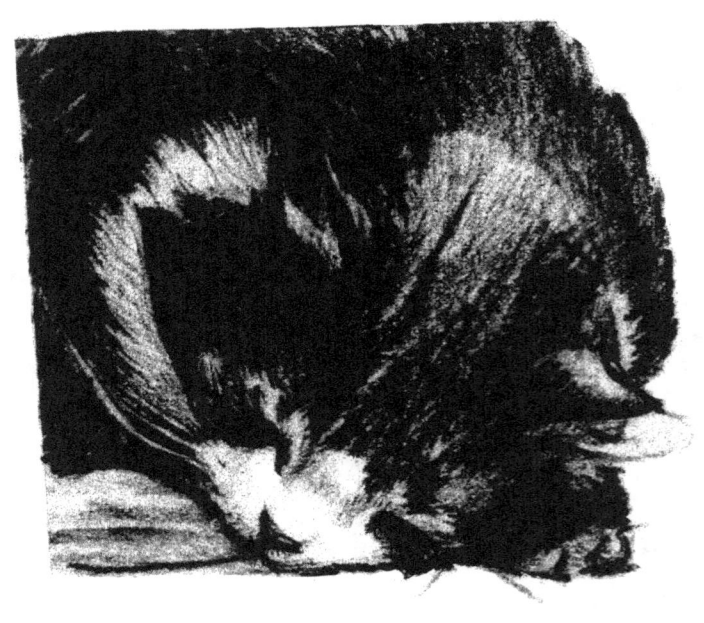

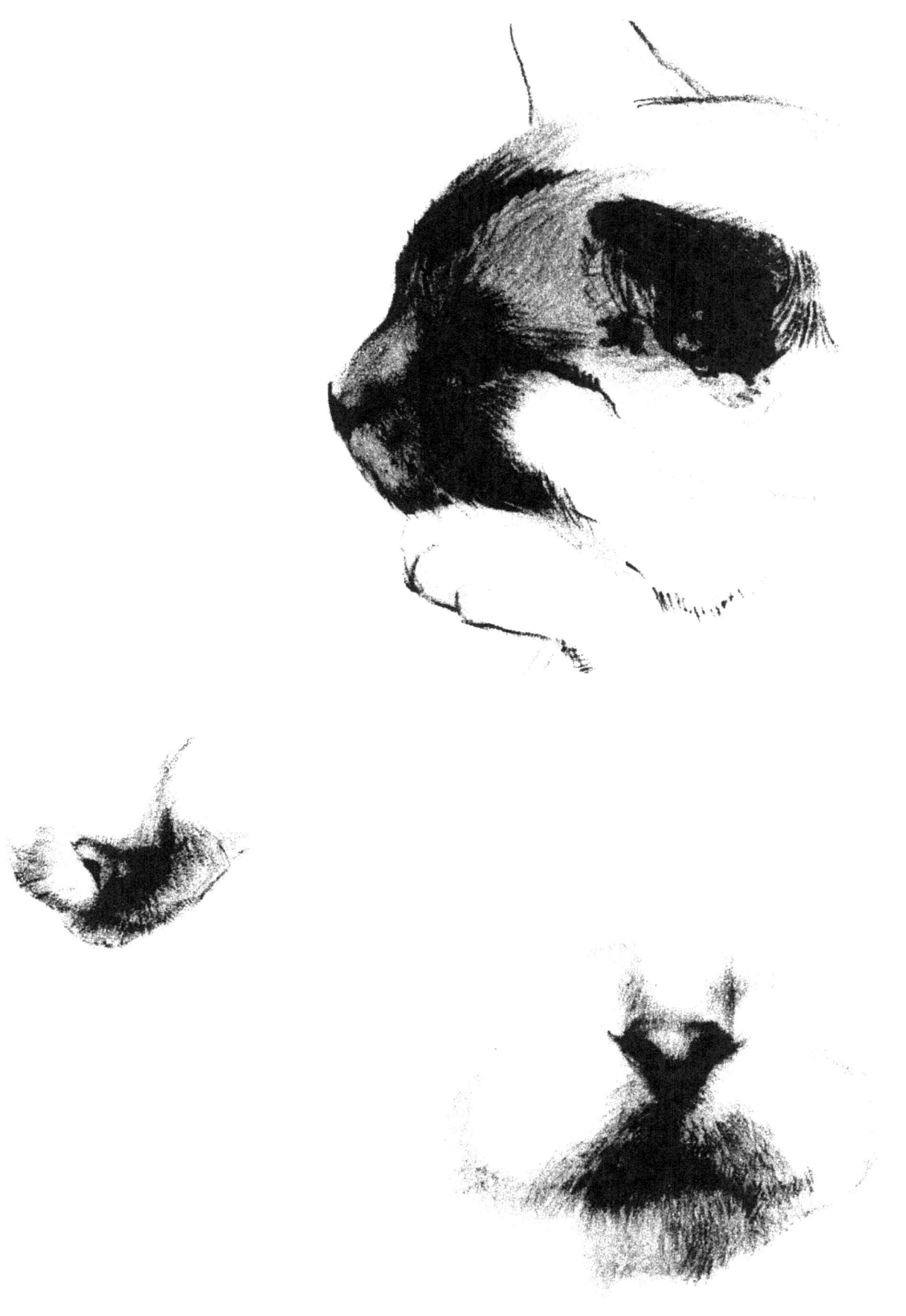

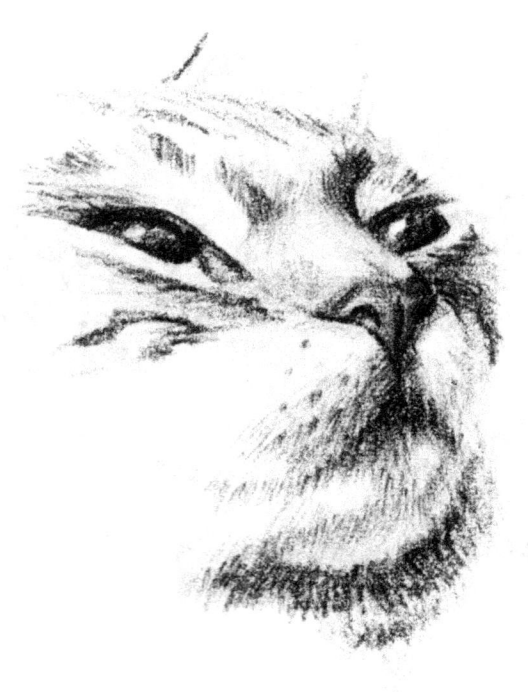

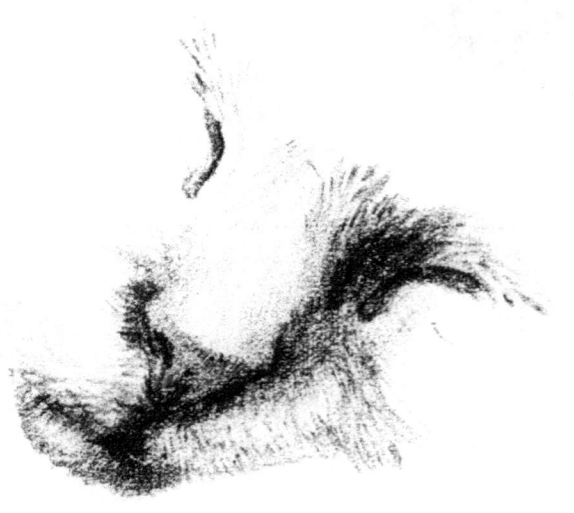

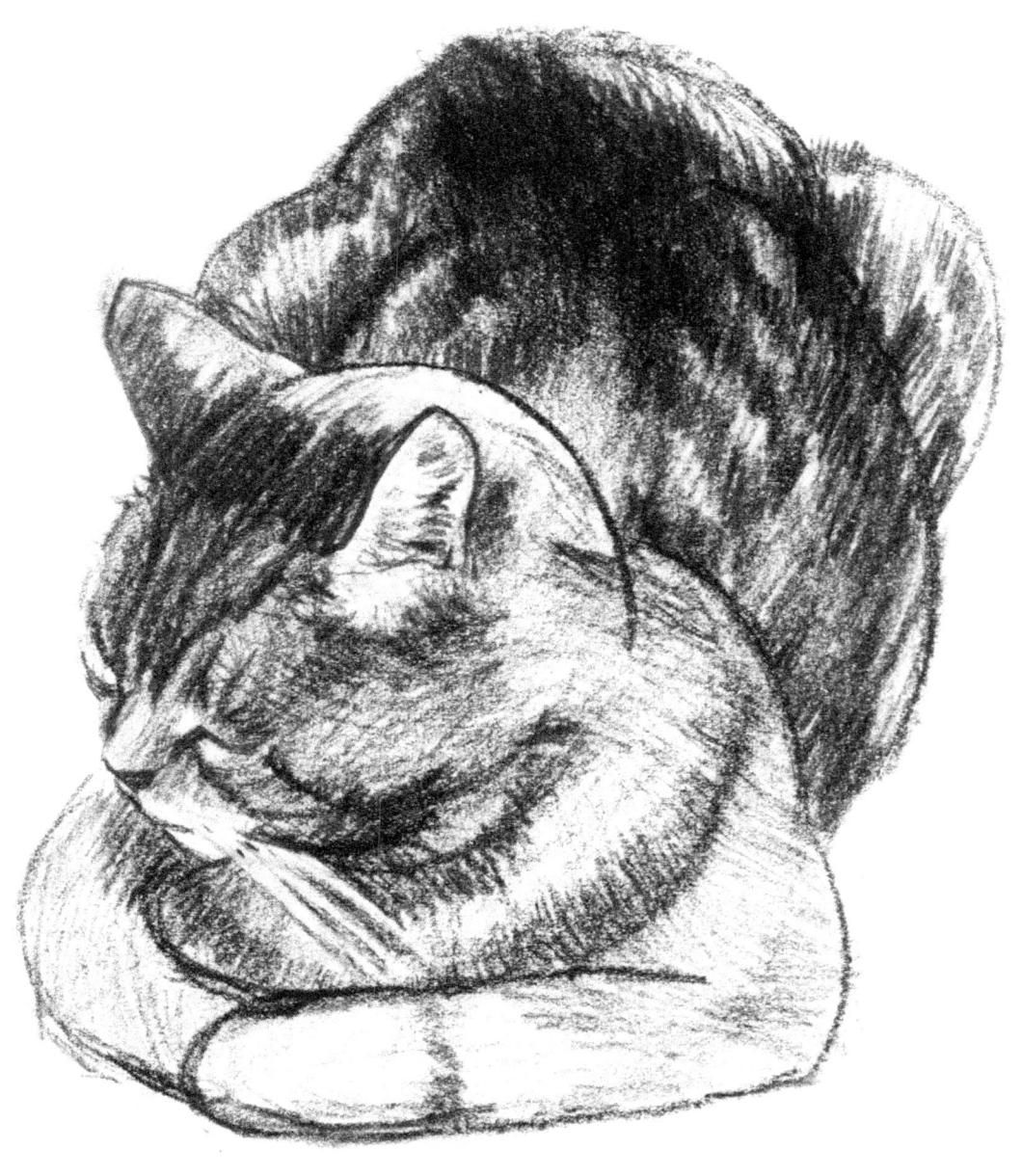

CIRCLES AND OVALS

The study above shows the advantage of circles and ovals for sketching in a rapid start for form, line and position, giving a solid base to build on. If your model continues in the same position you can begin refining and adding the character of the definite features, the texture of fur and the markings.

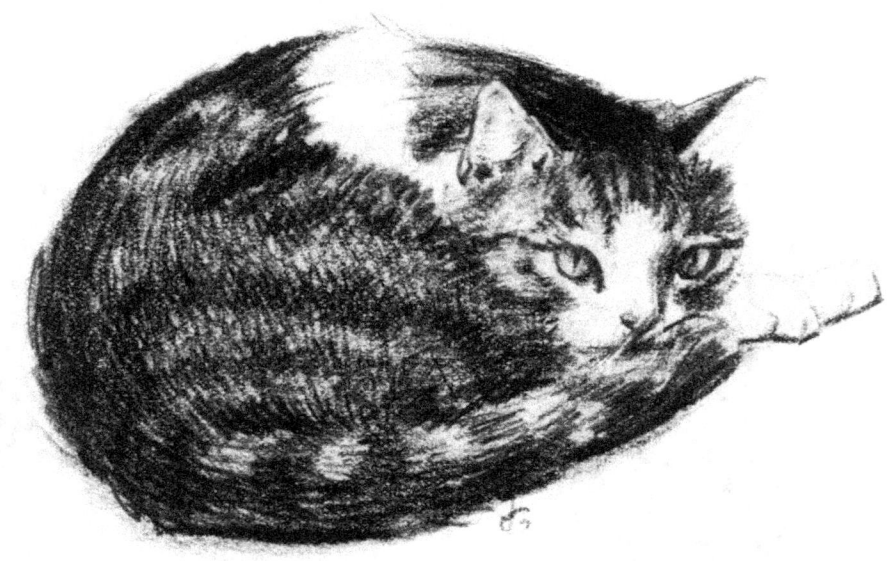

CAUTION

The two sketches here again show how the circles and ovals can first be applied and the bearing that the marking has on portraiture.

The portrait head shows why the pencil point must be sharp when this medium, the lithograph pencil is used from the start of this sketch to the finish. It is well to remember how difficult it is to erase the lithograph crayon and it is best to be careful to make a very light sketch to start using the number four and number one at the finish. Have a watchful eye to see that your marks go where you want them and as you meant them. It is real disaster to make a beautiful picture only to have it ruined by a careless stroke at the finish.

It is most important to leave the white paper for the whites and the white whiskers or feelers which melt into the white fur but show distinctly against the dark fur.

When you turn to the page of paws and forearms note the careful study of the construction, take your cat's paws in your hand and study the direction of the fur on the outside and the protective way it grows between the toes and pads underneath. Notice the quaintness of the paws with the extra toes. Notice how the nails are placed, it may seem a small thing to do, but to know your subject is very worth while.

Have you ever examined the cat's tail for the beauty of design in the markings?

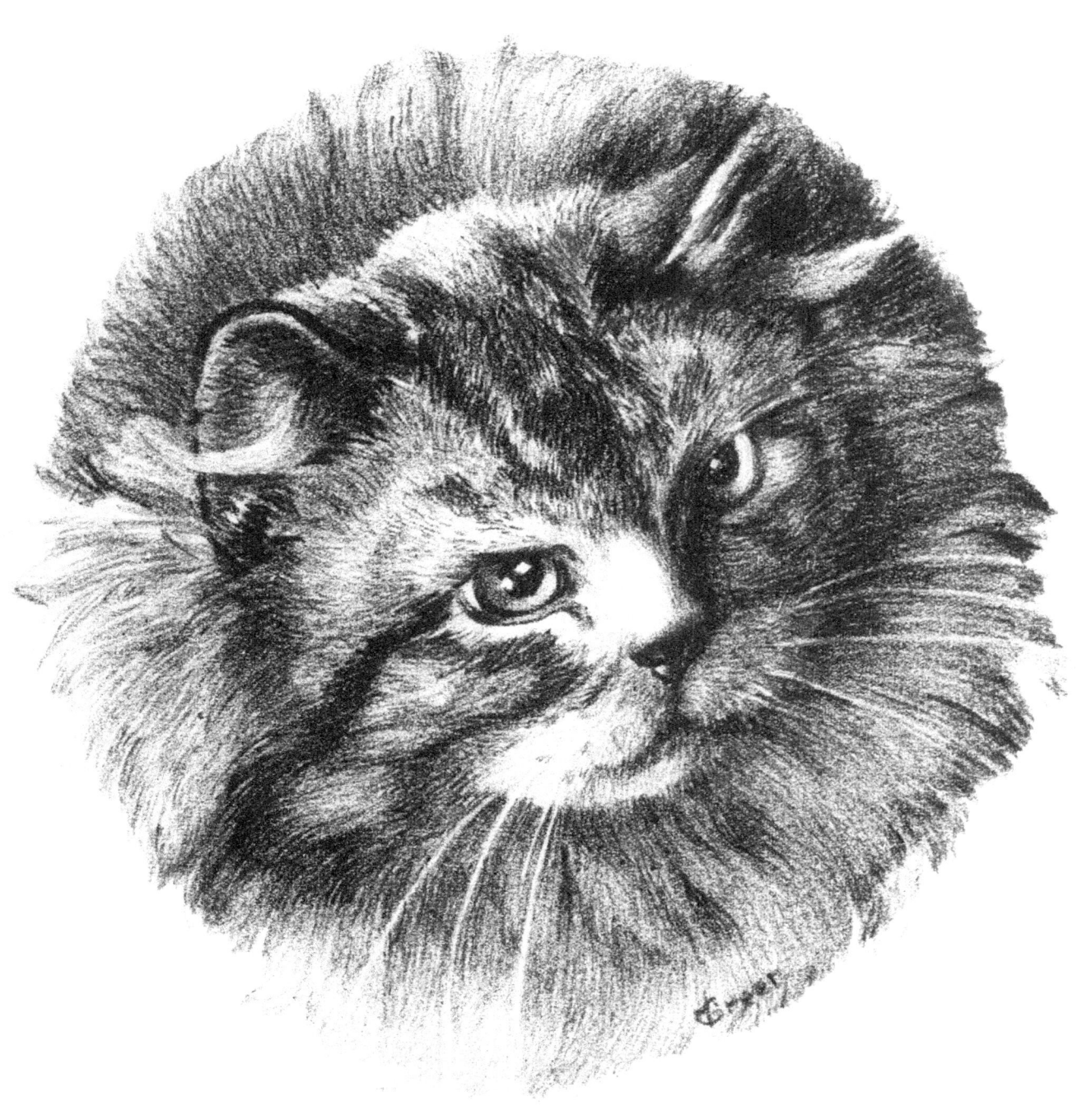

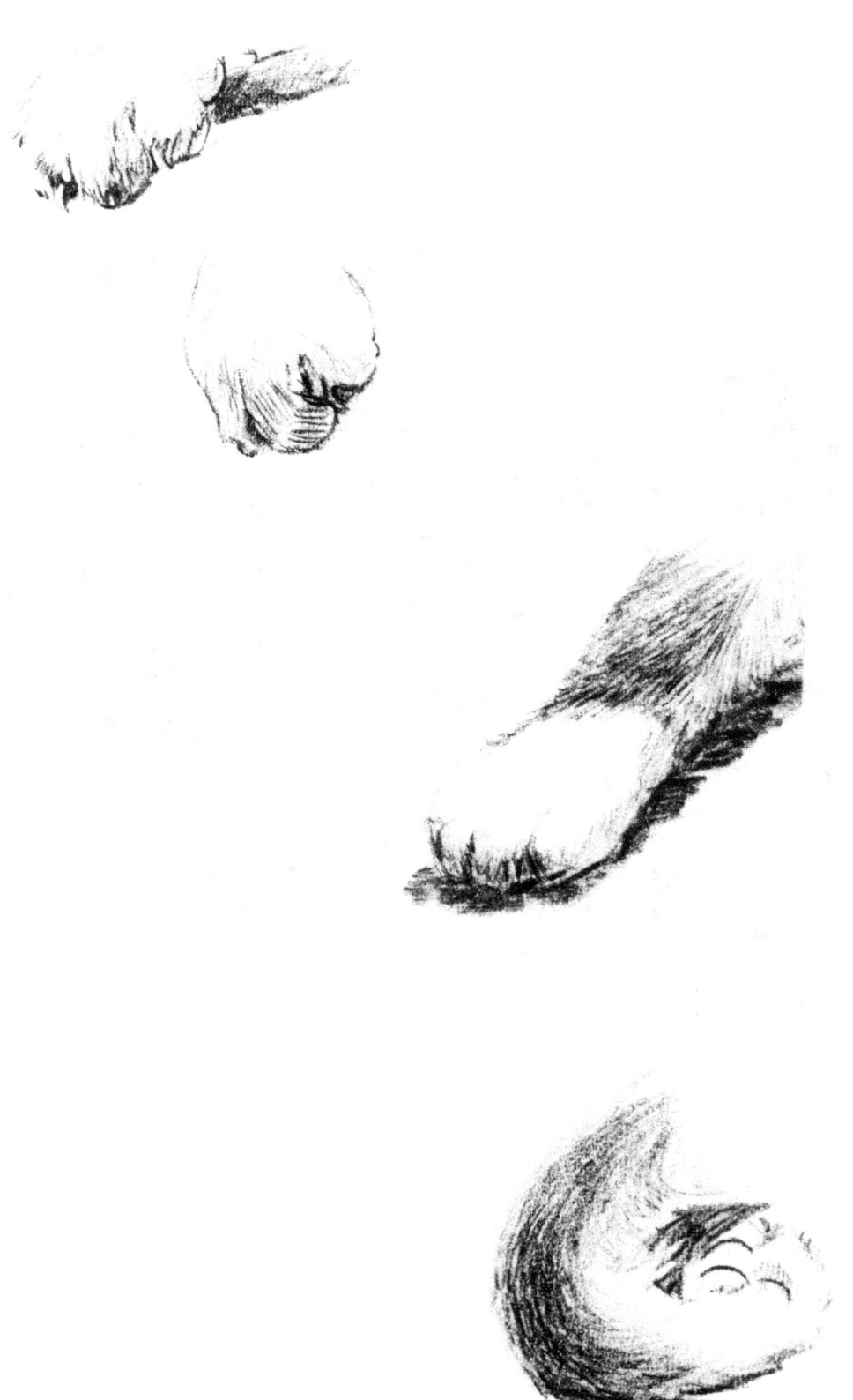

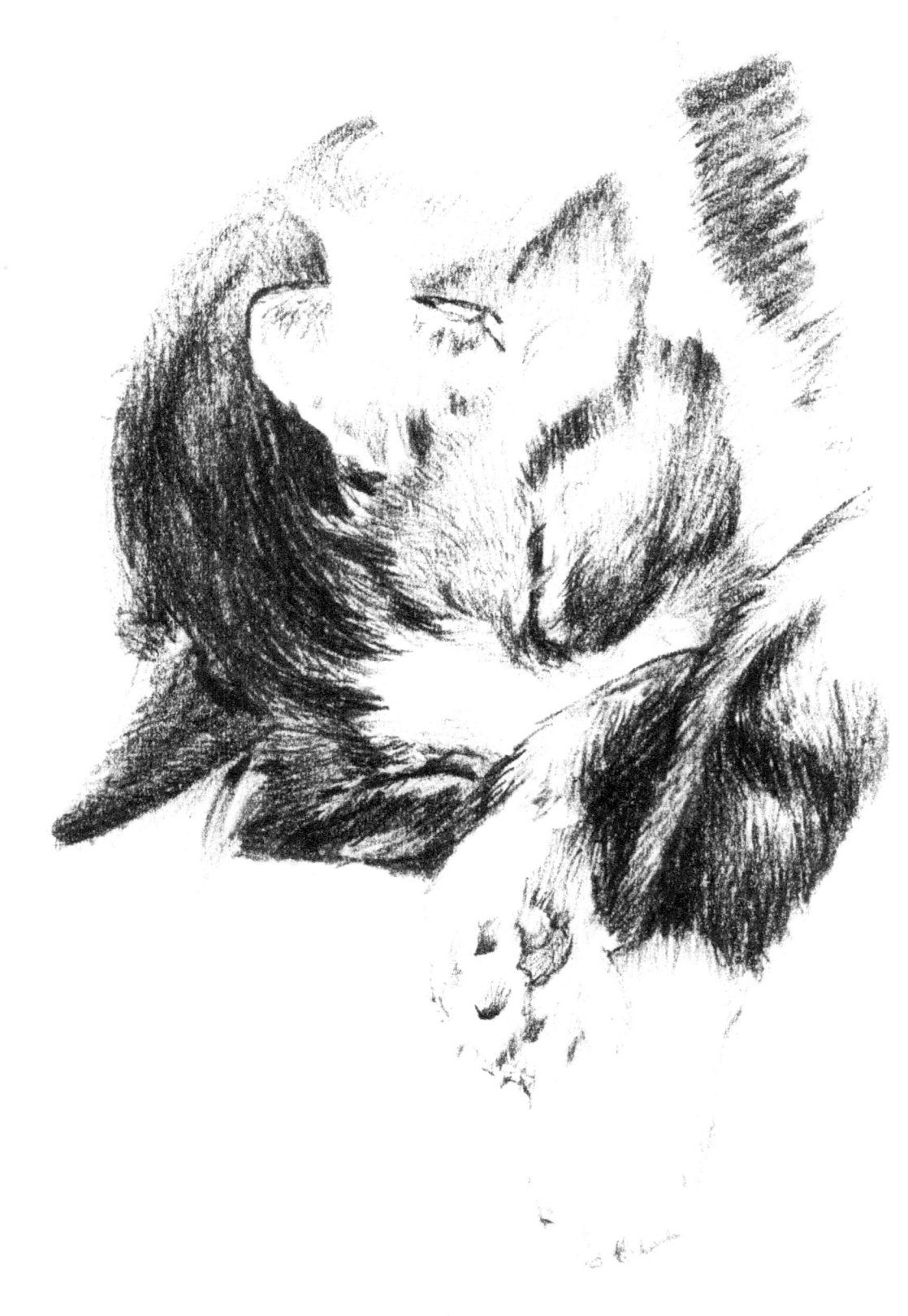

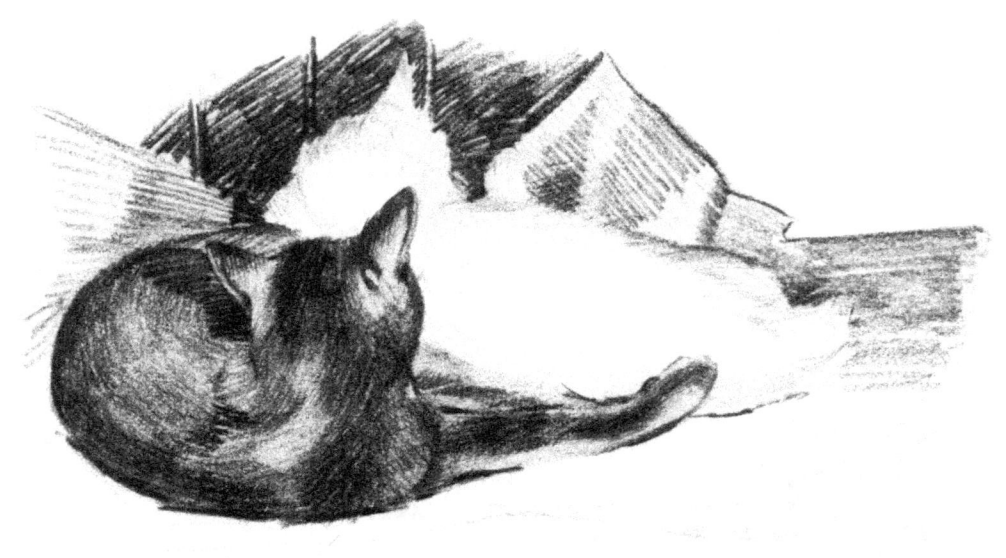

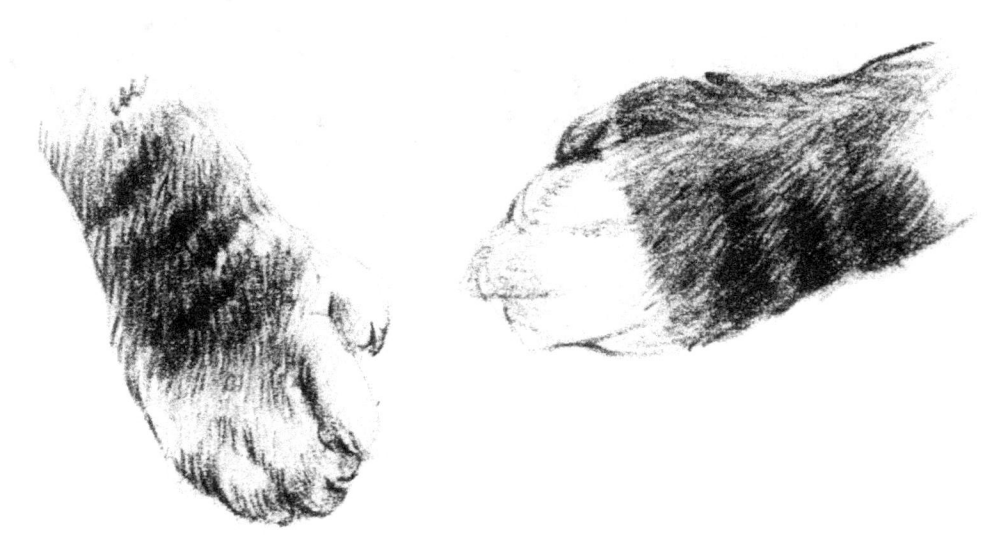

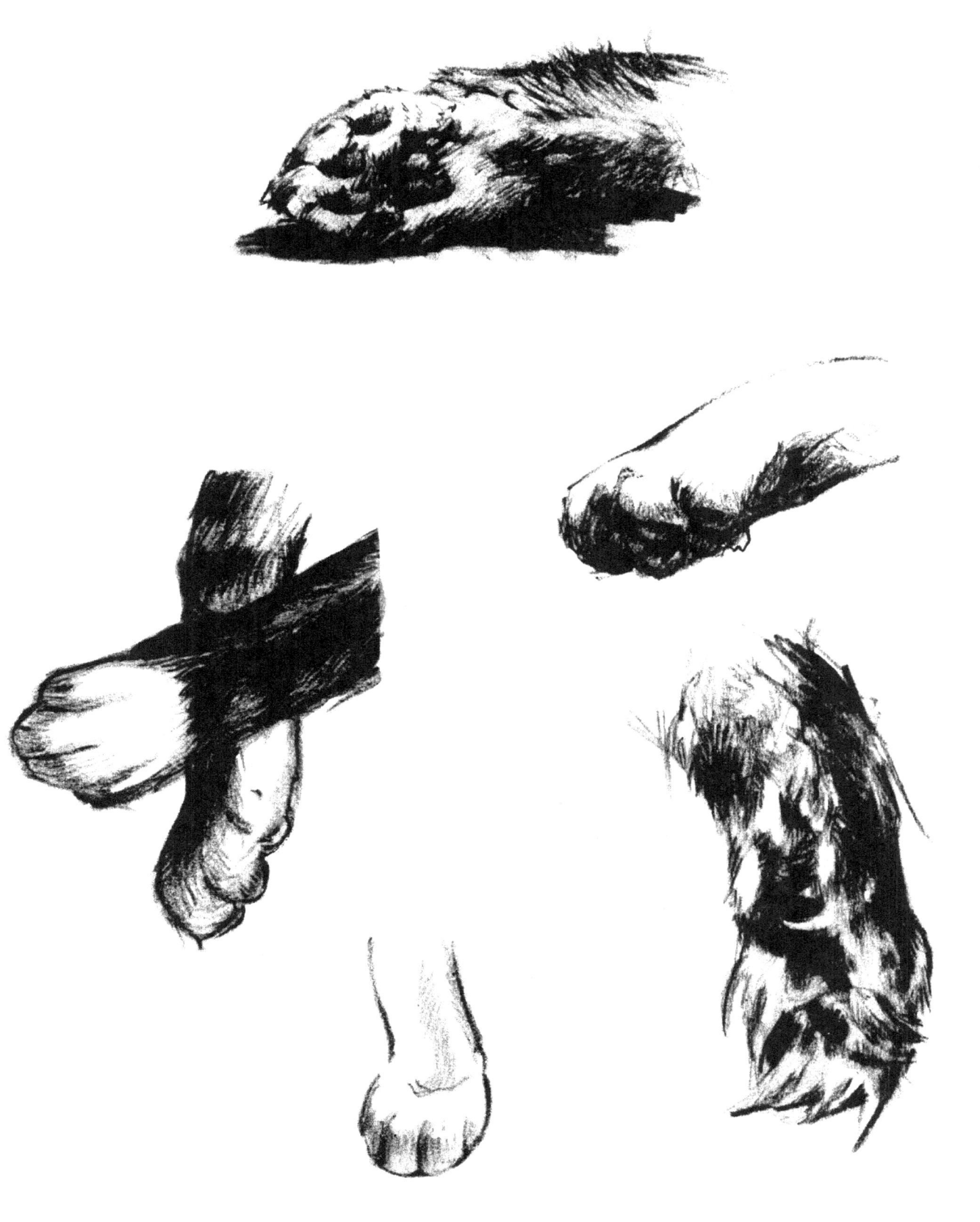

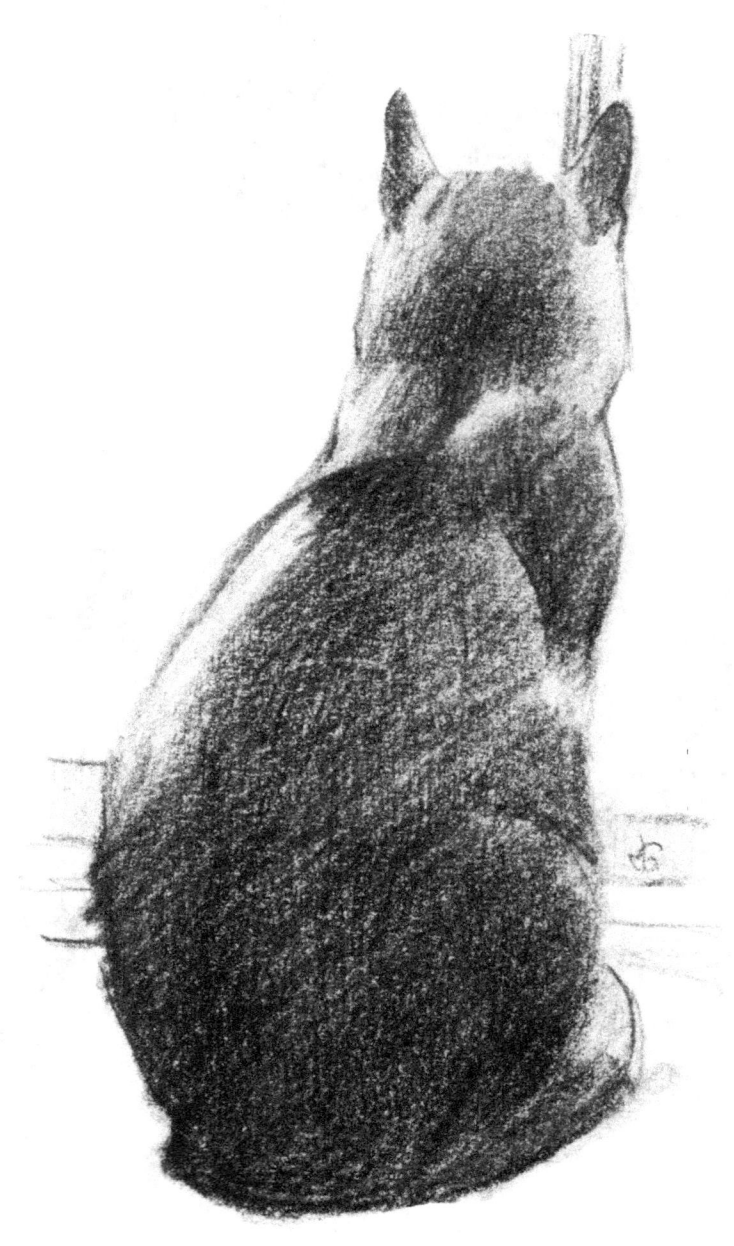

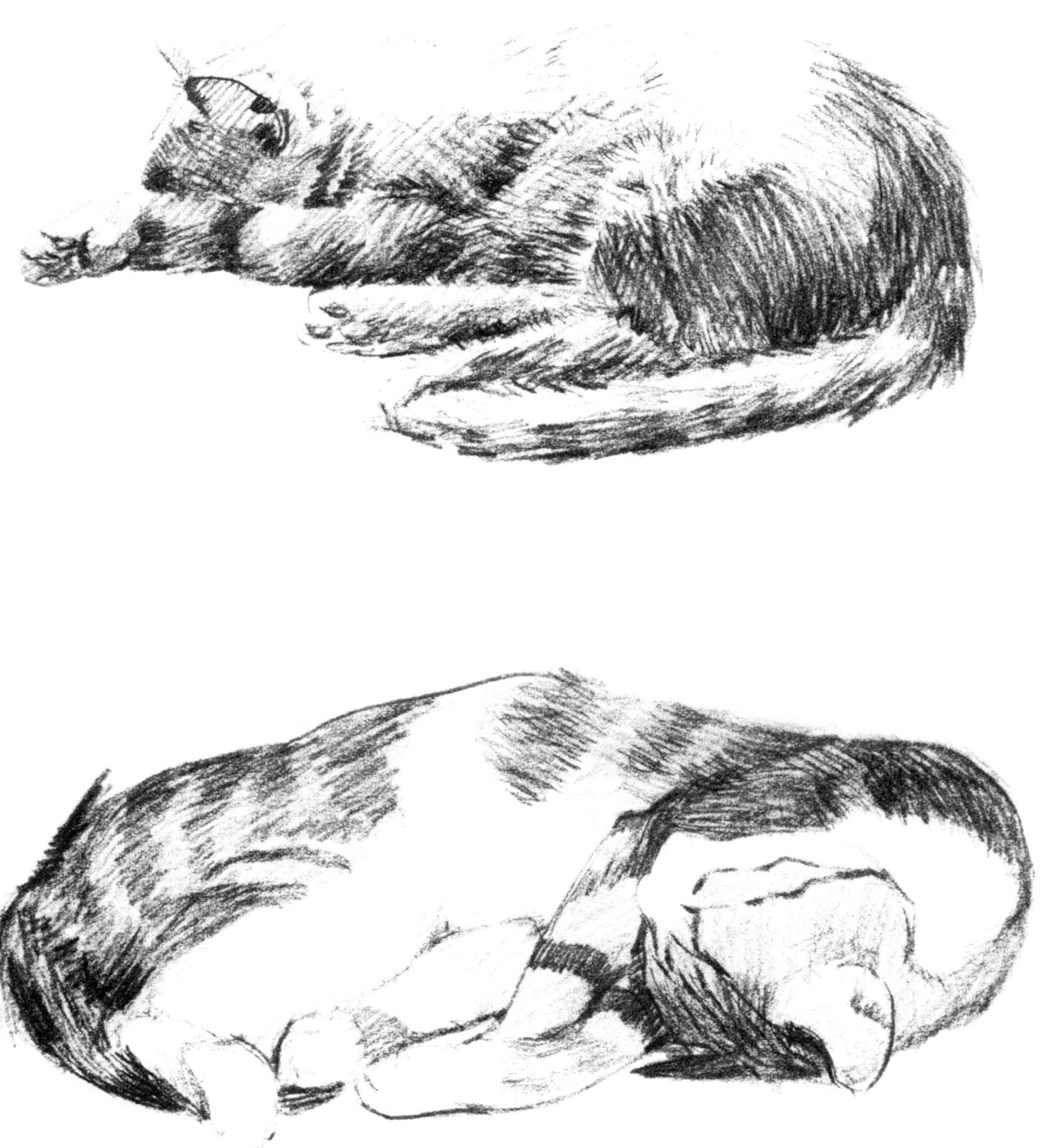

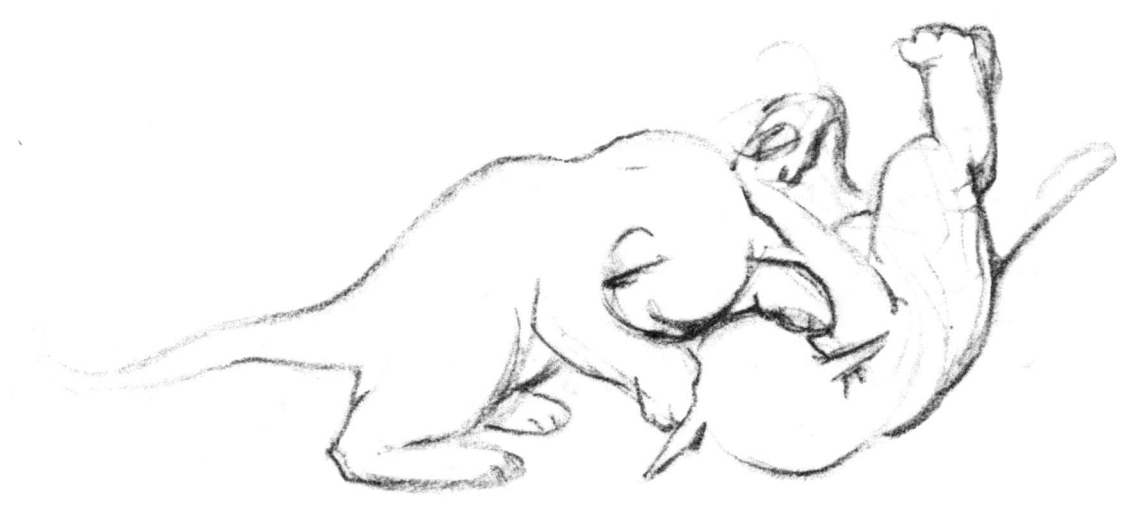

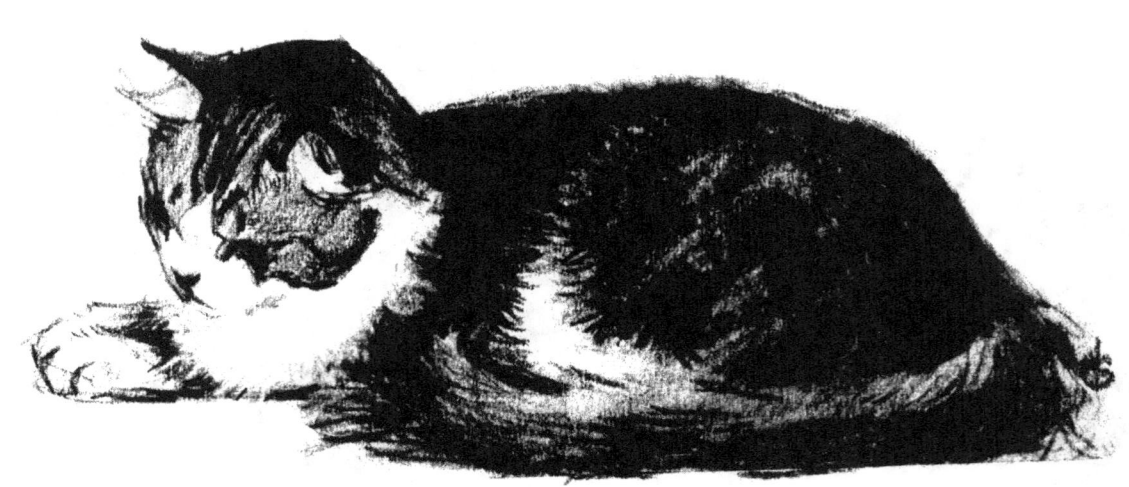

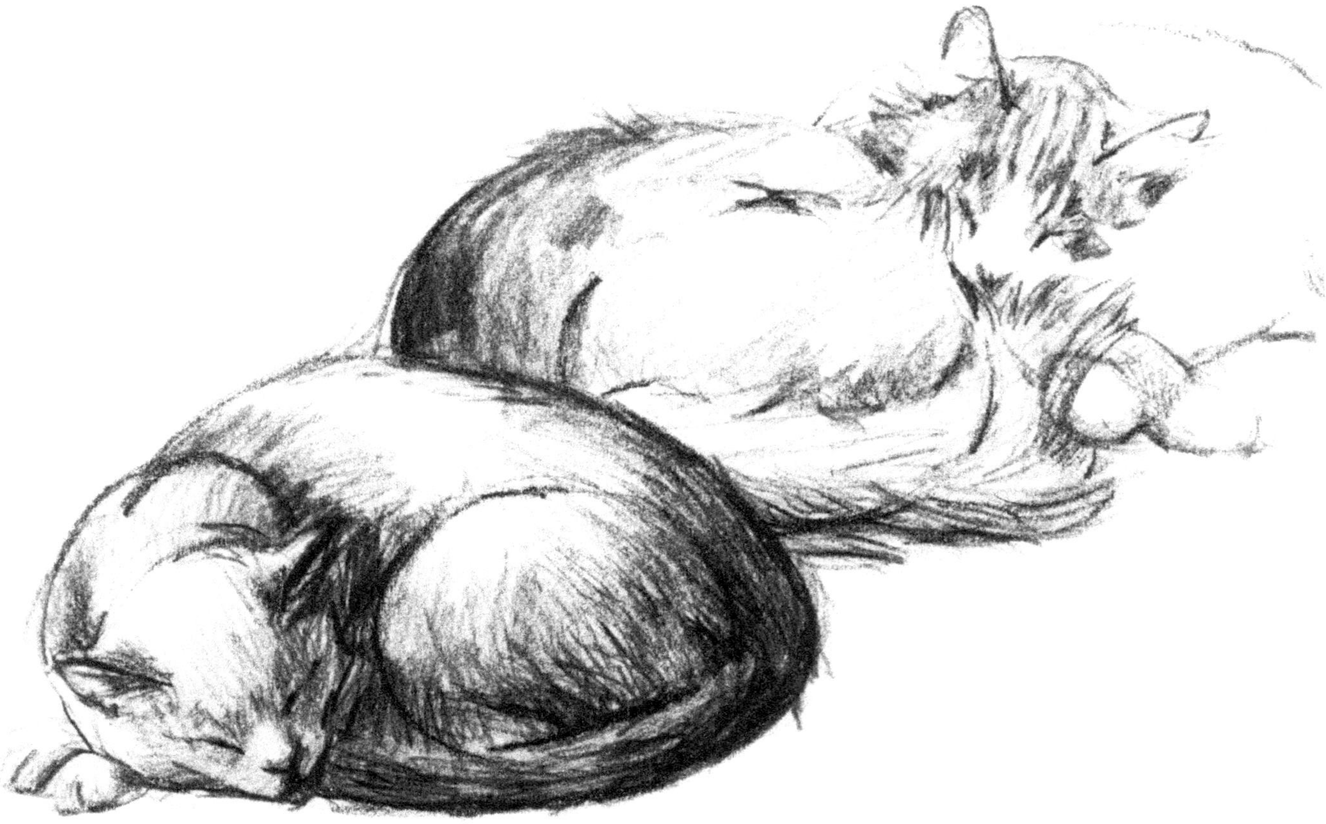

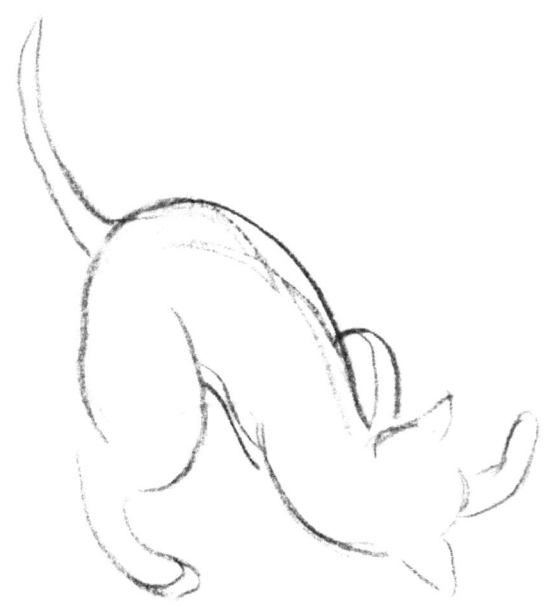

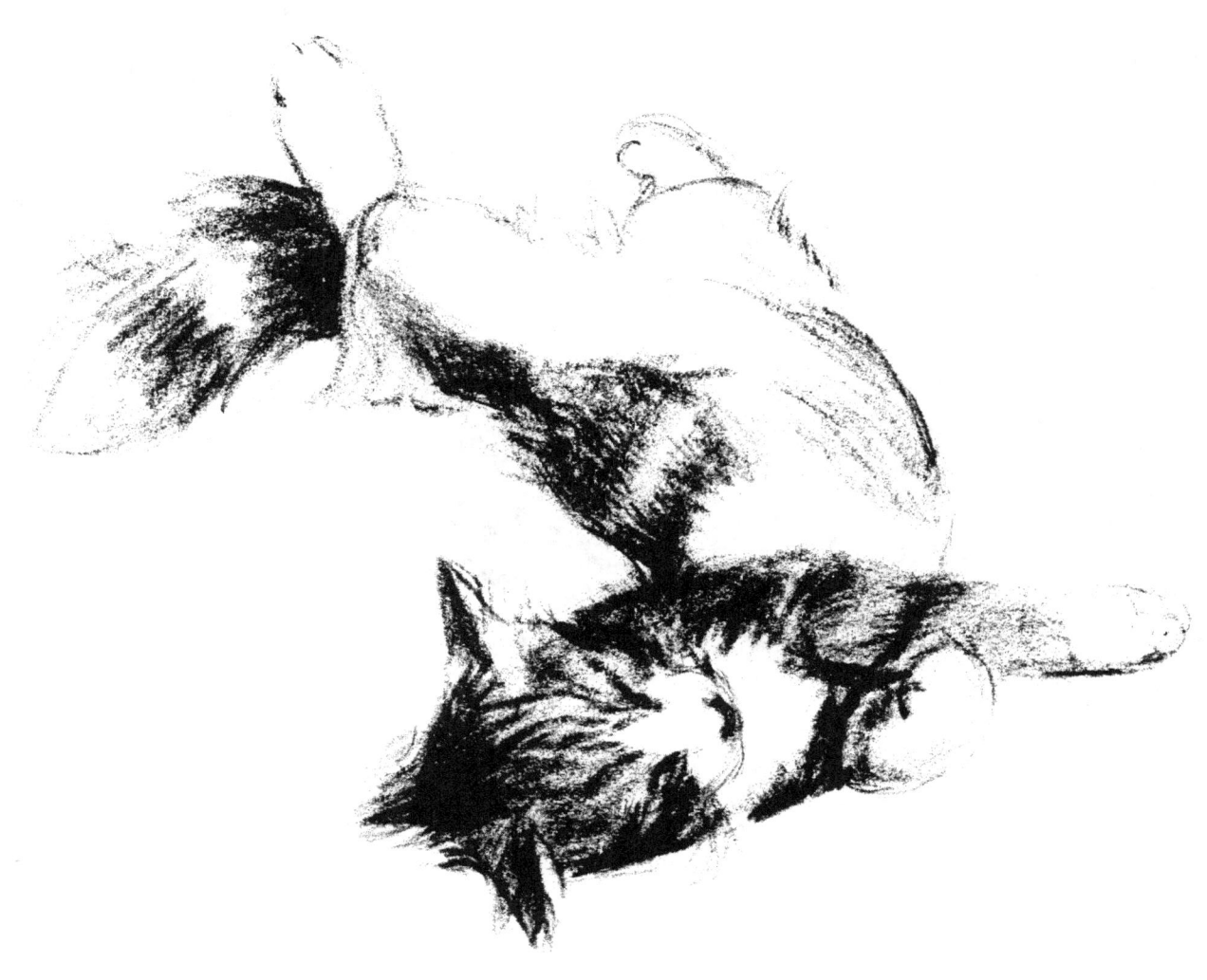

CHARMING PERSONALITIES

Young Topaze in his siesta is an alluring picture with the ever graceful line and youthful contours, unselfconscious, unaware of the appeal he makes to any person.

Topaze is of brilliant red orange coloring with snowy white and orange colored eyes, a subject worthy of any brush.

The little coquette below is a pure white Persian floating along like down when she walks with an air about her that says she can do no wrong.

Close association and a vast amount of study of the cats develops your perception of their individual charm and personality.

In a group of cats of varied ages have you remarked the sweet gentleness of the older cats with the younger kittens and the love and faith in every line of the kitten for the older cat?

Cats love to cuddle and bunch up for company as well as warmth. A cluster of cats sketched at this time makes an unusual collection of studies to refer to.

All one color or hues of the same value make a very settled sketch, while a group of different colors develop into a very dynamic sketch.

Cats at their beauty treatments are always interesting and present countless numbers of graceful studies. Never have I seen an awkward cat.

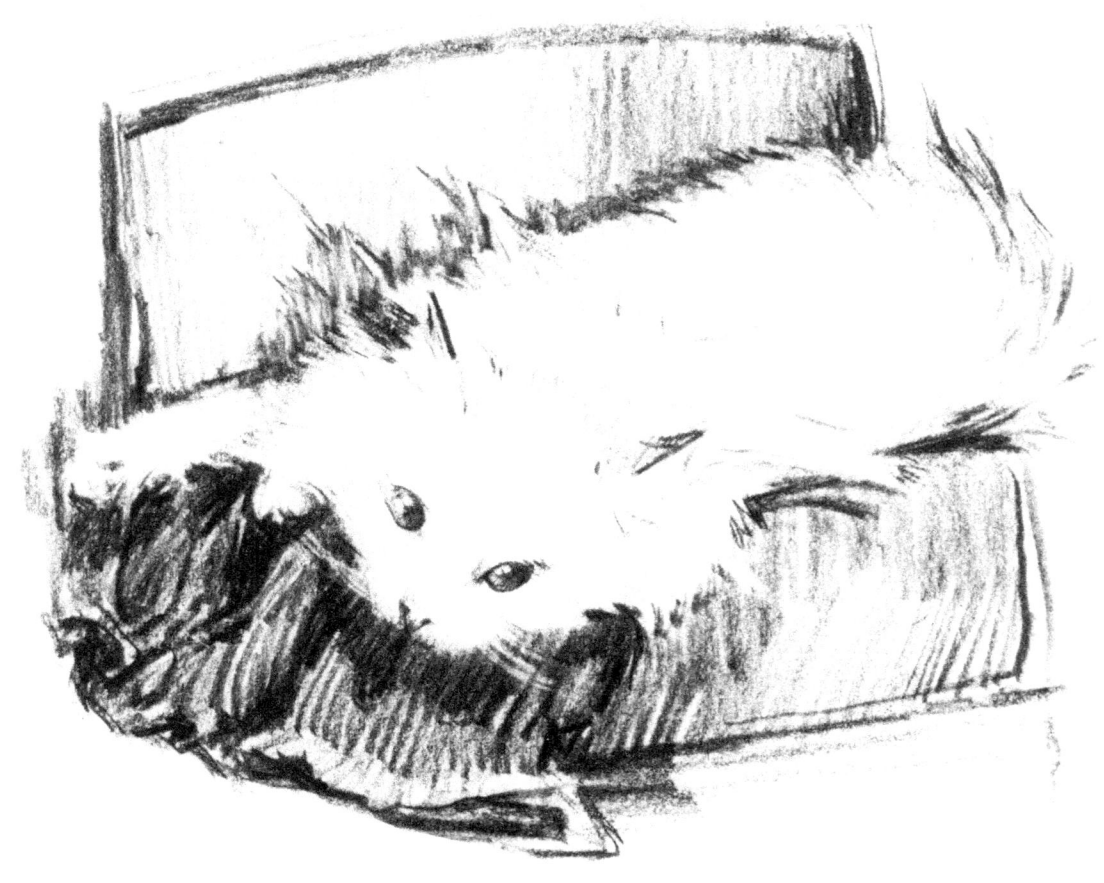

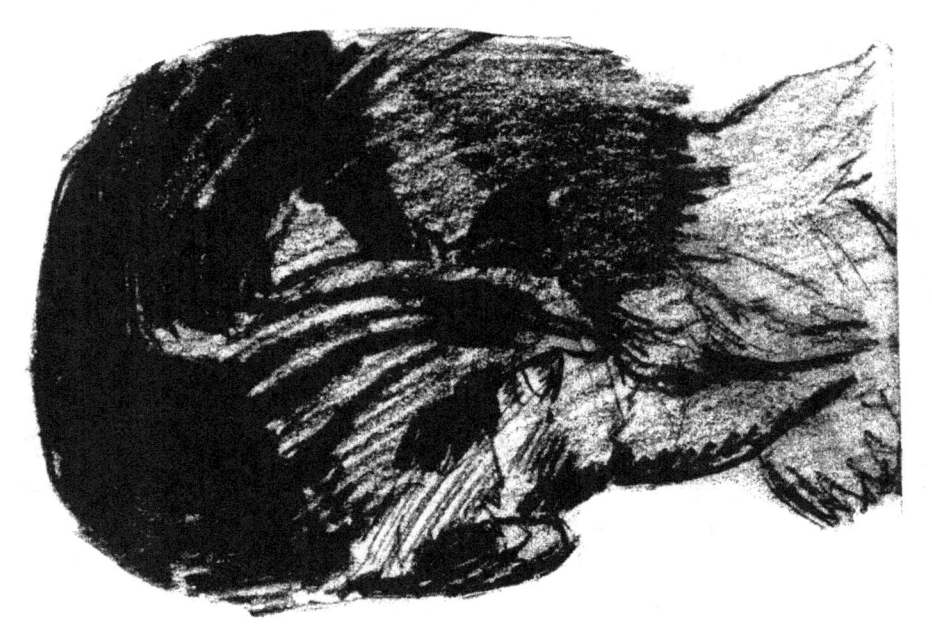

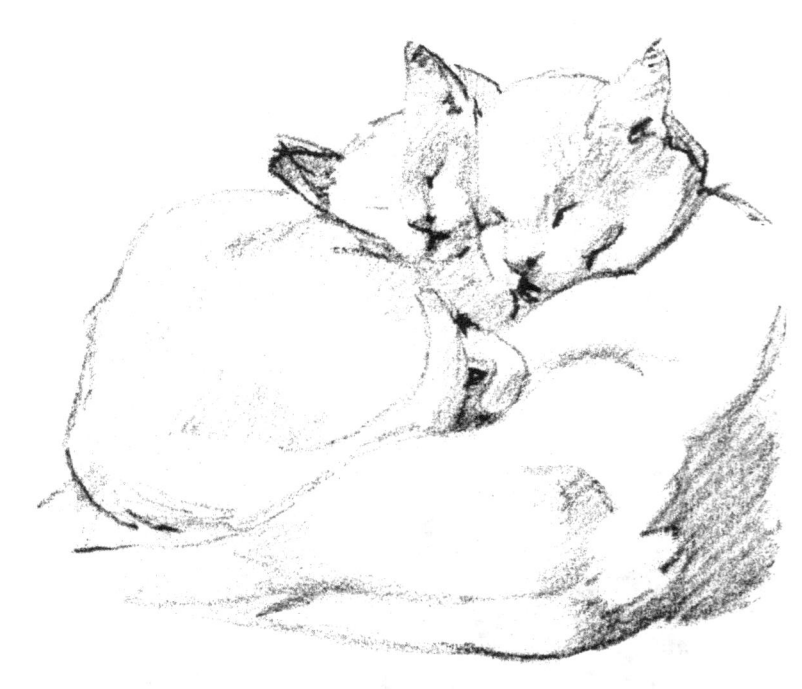

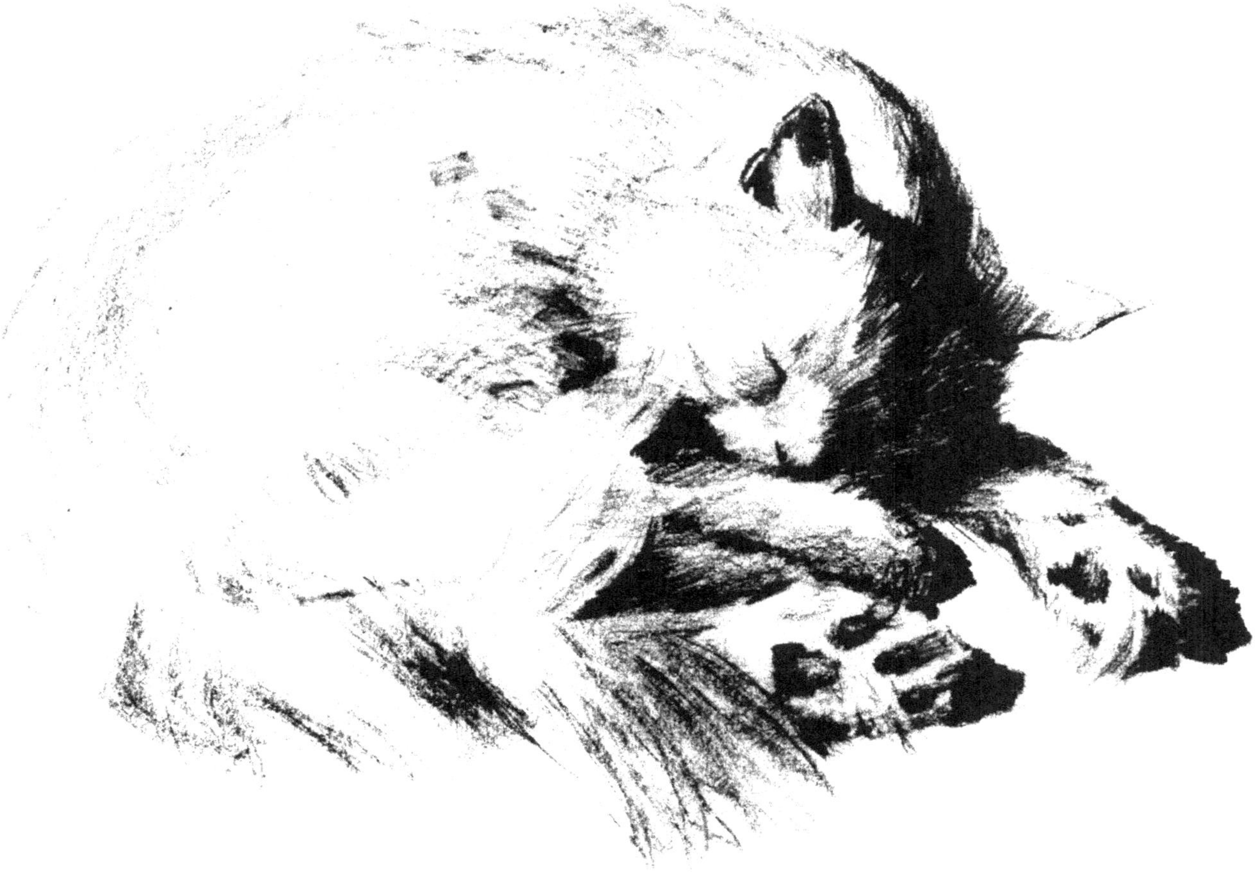

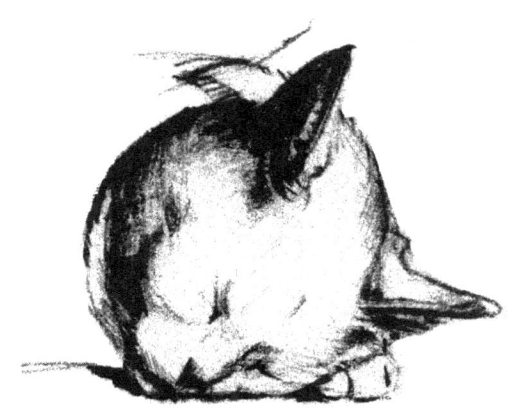

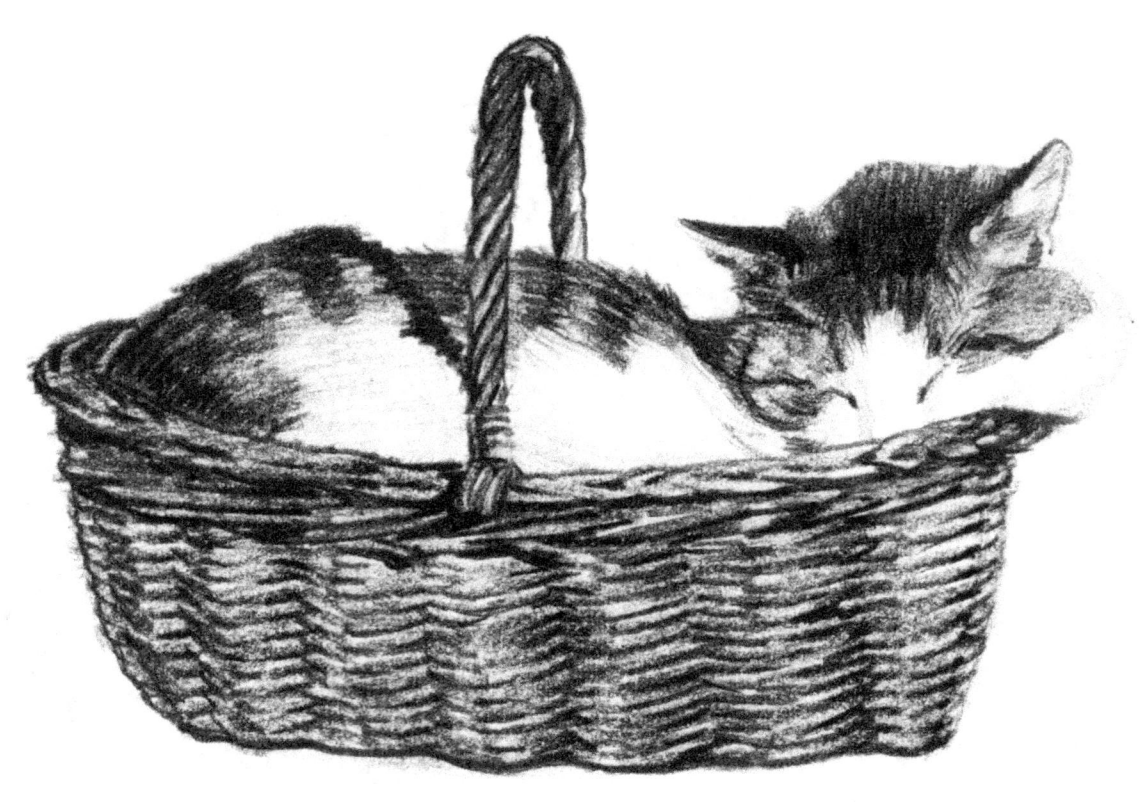

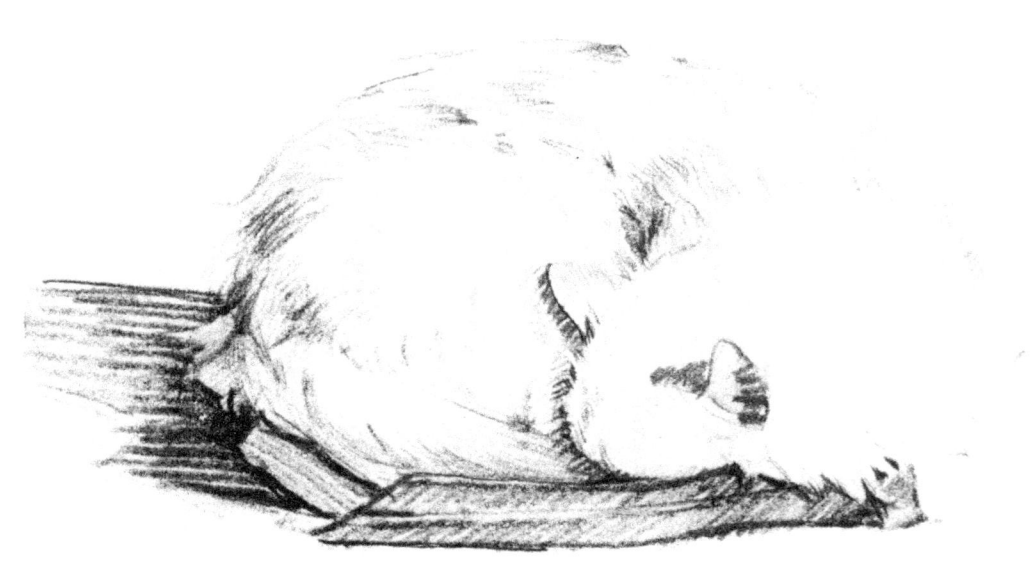

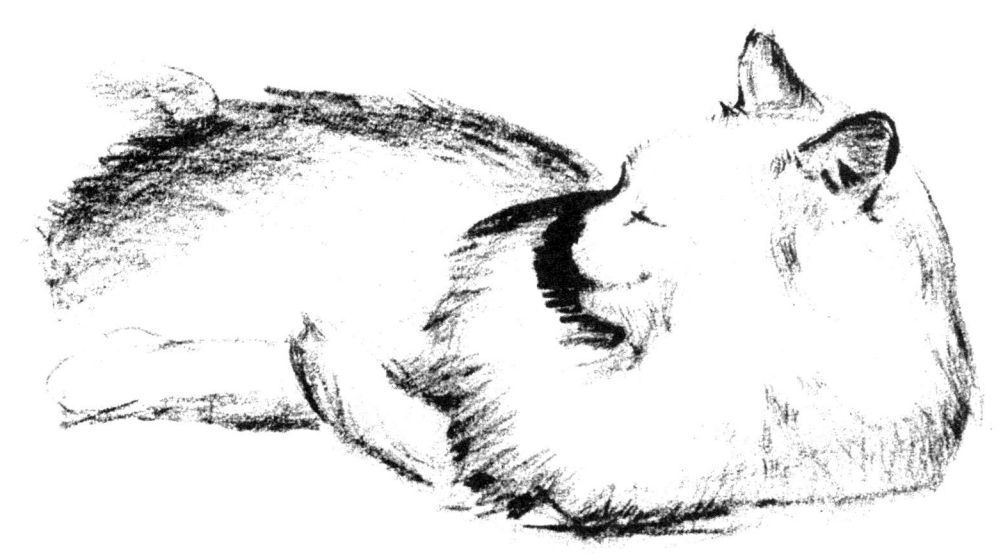

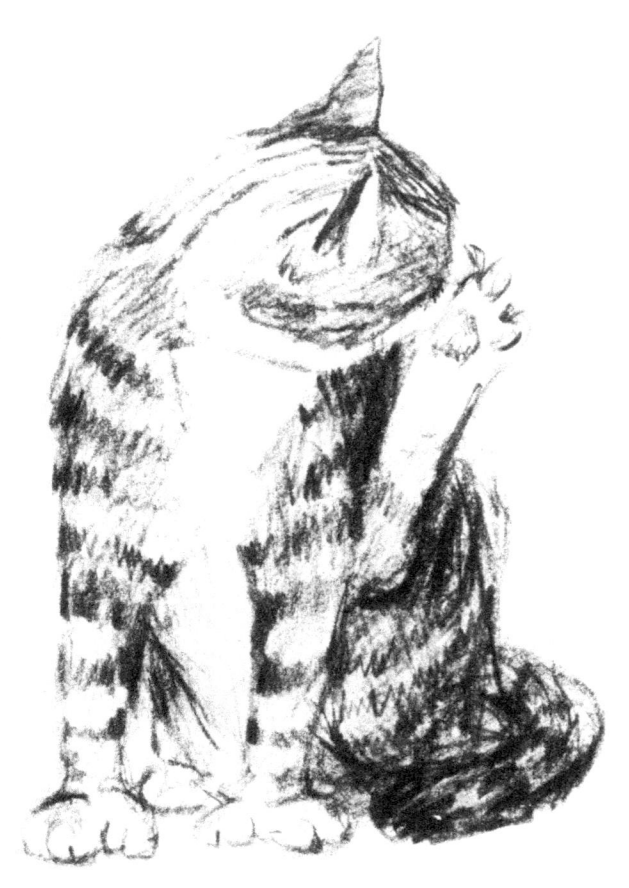

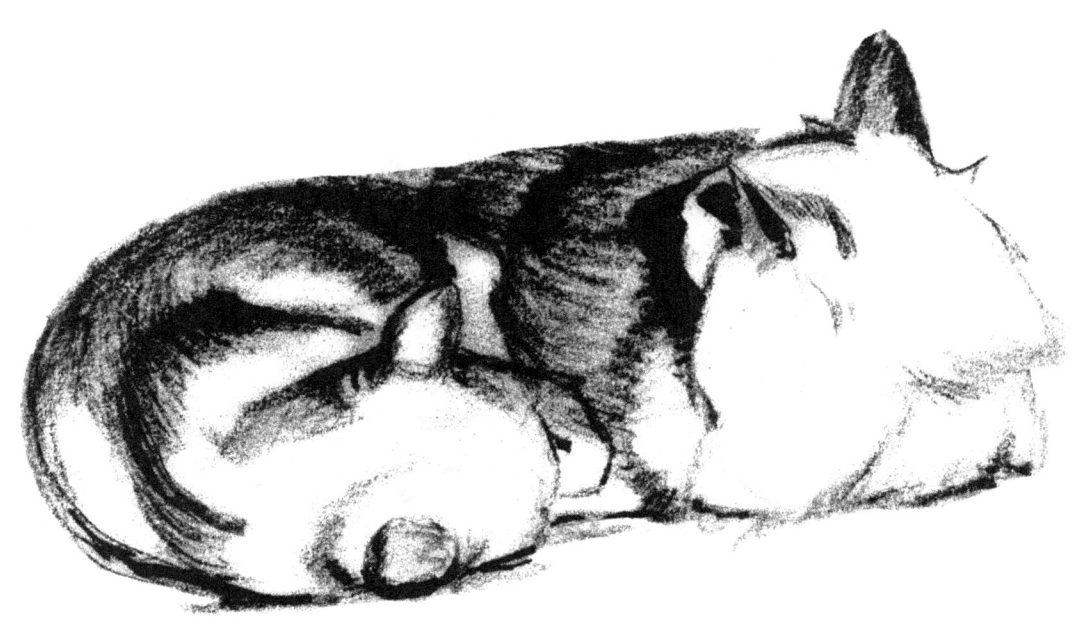

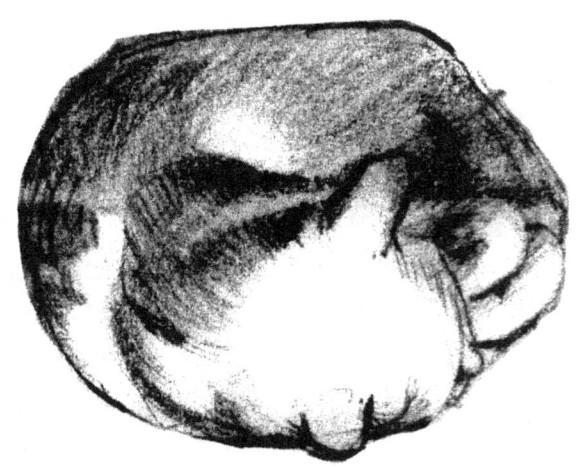

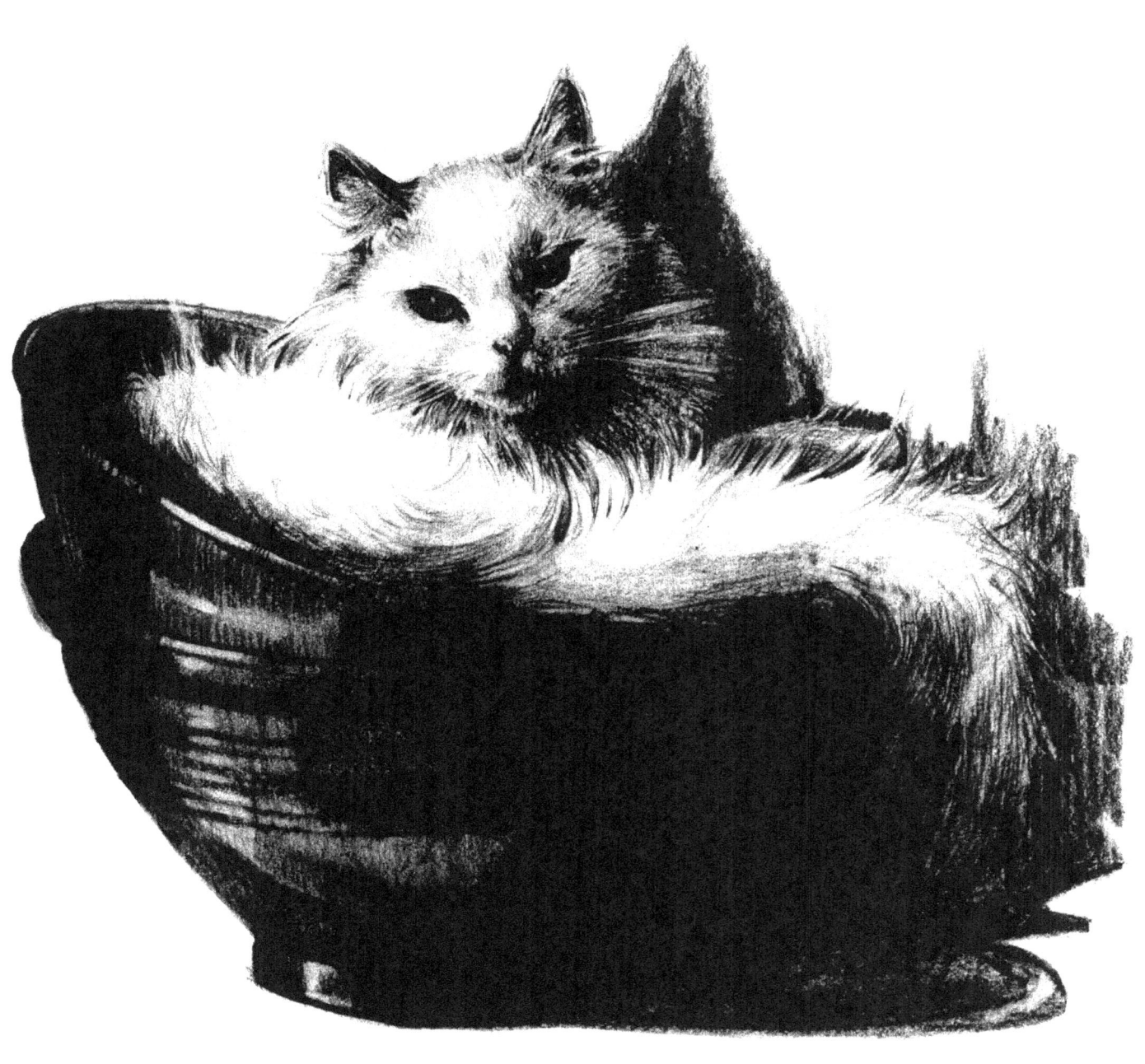

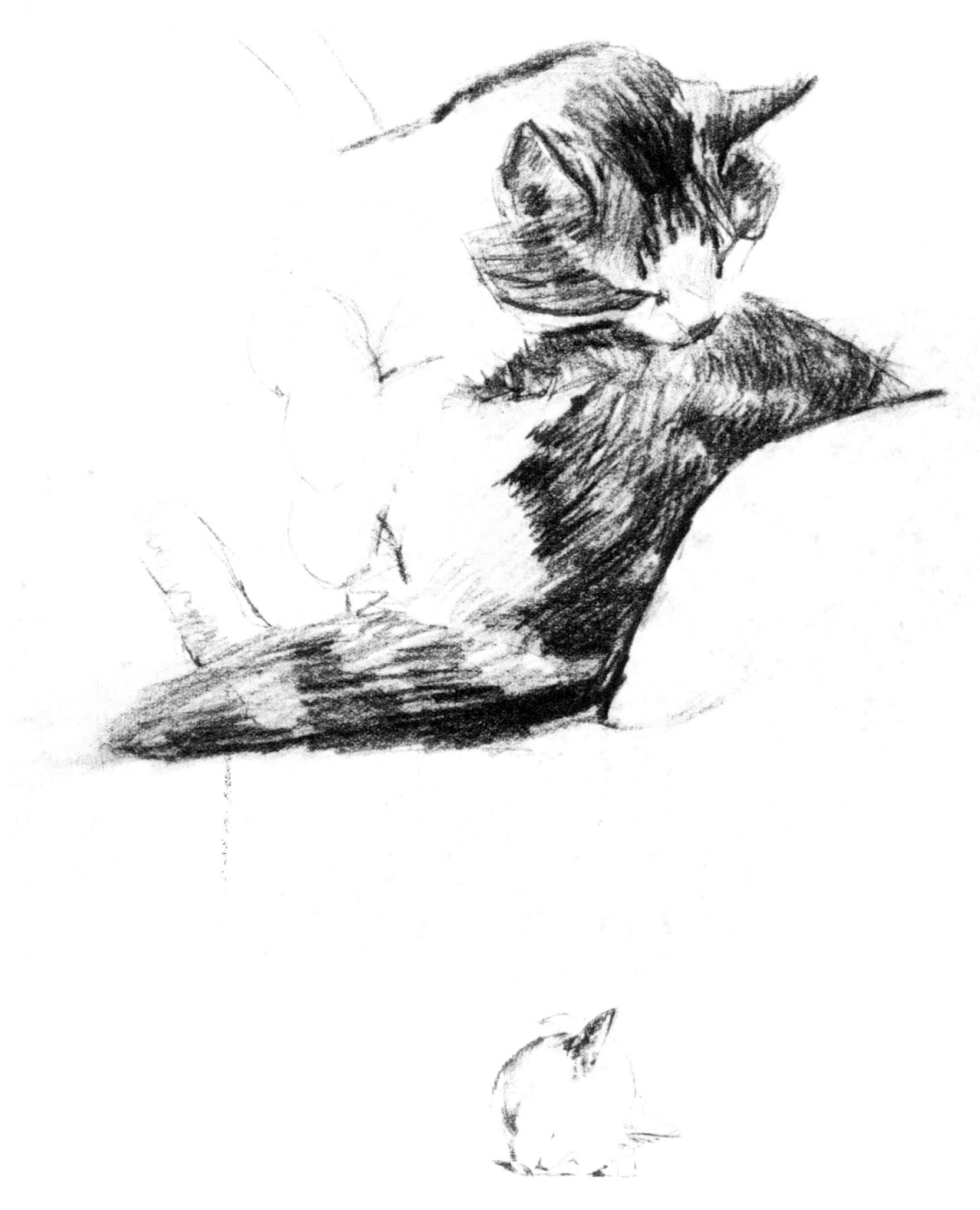

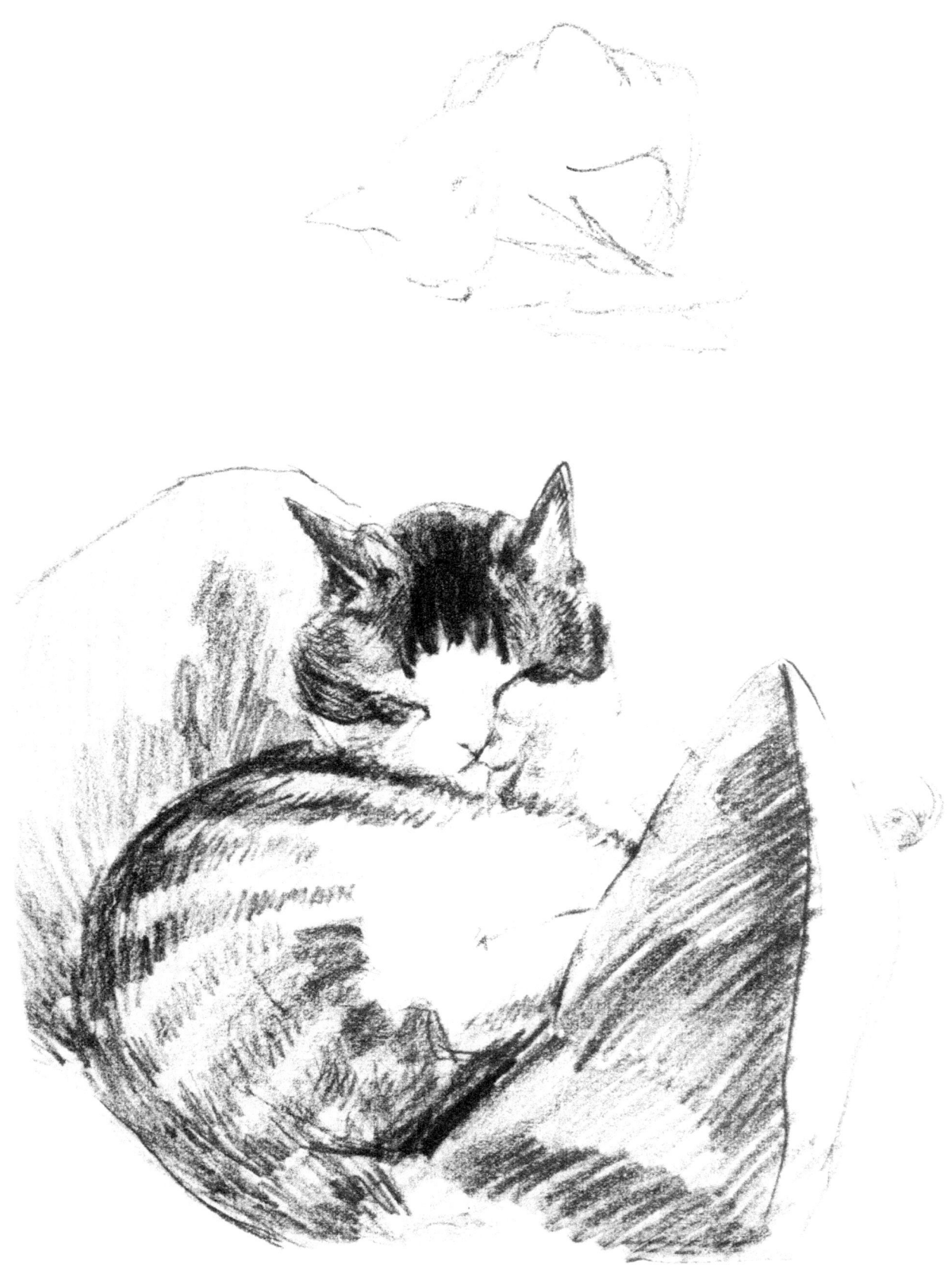

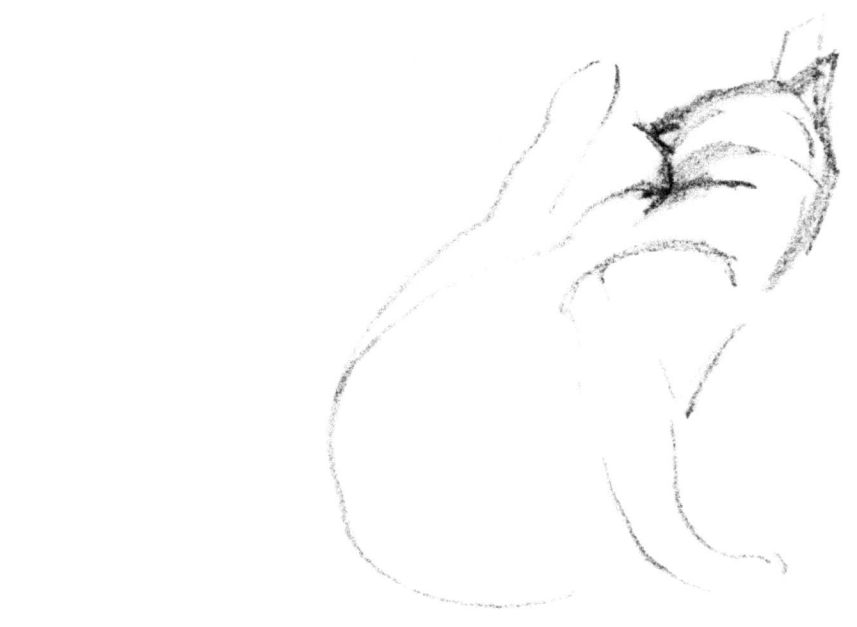

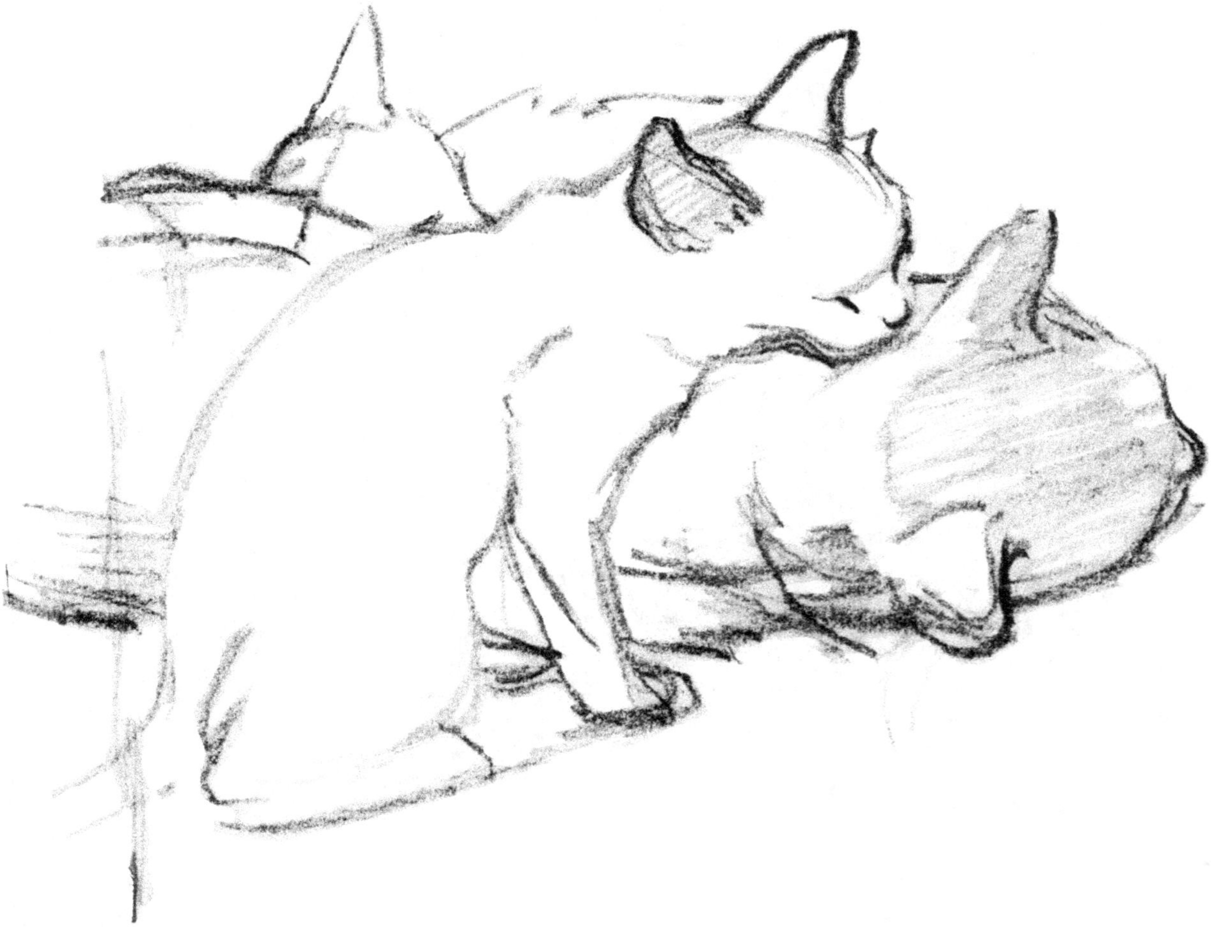

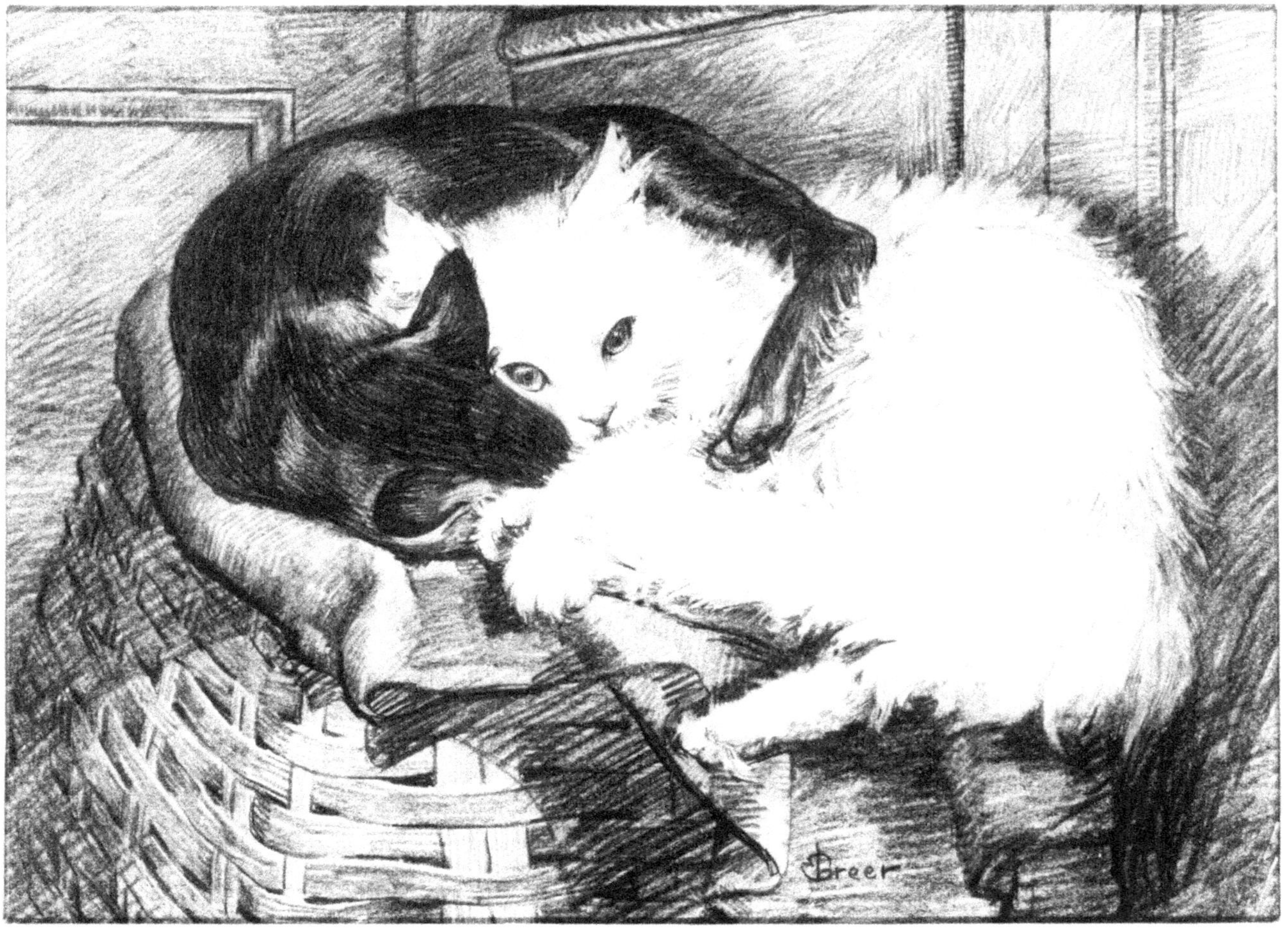

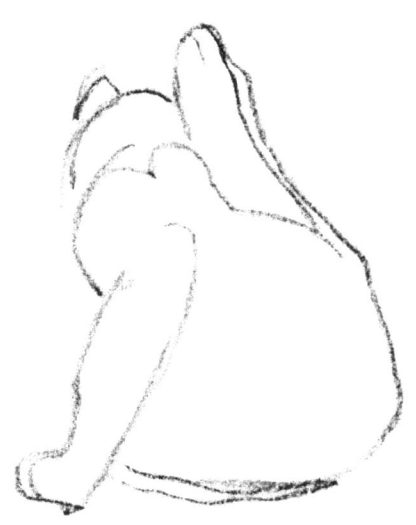

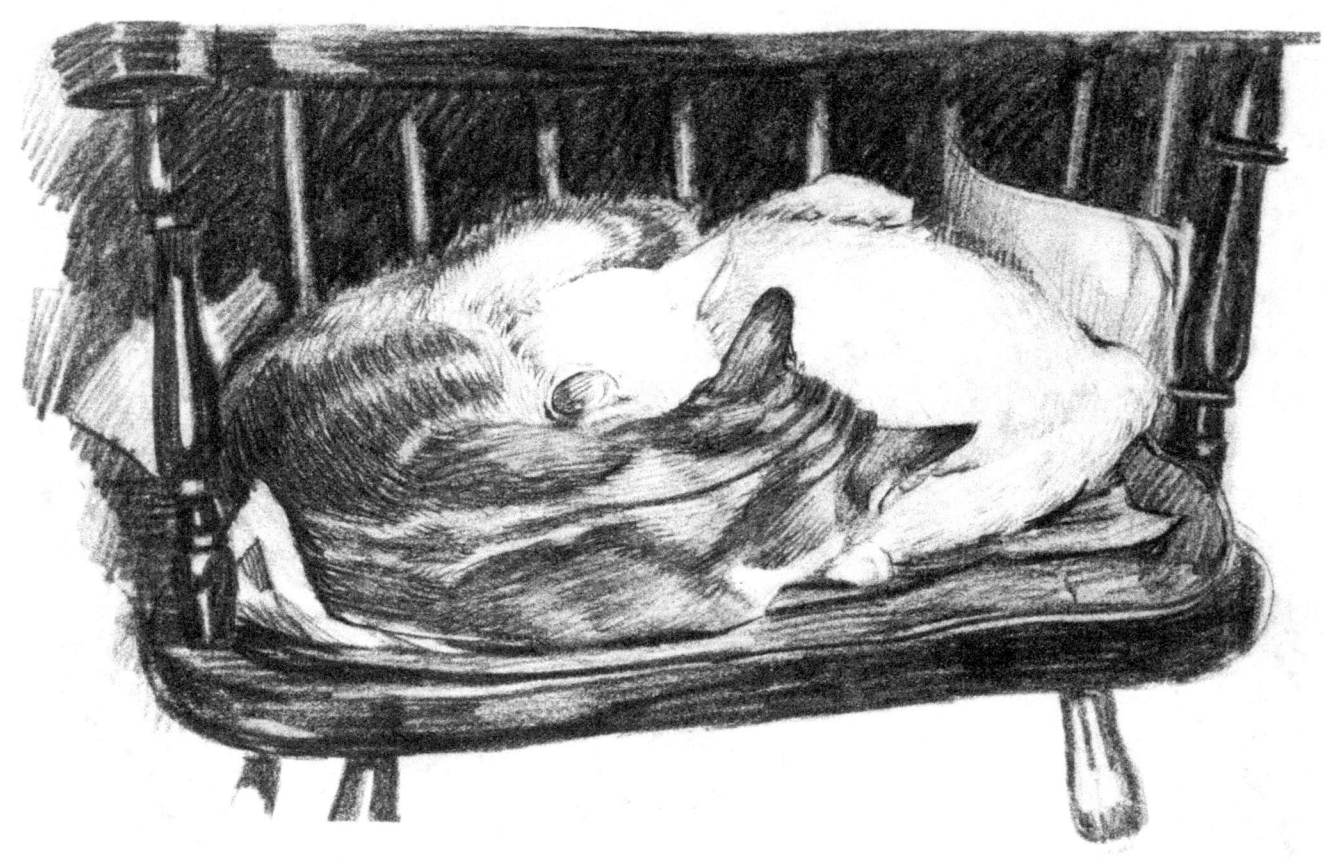

GROUPS

Groups are a real treat to work on. Put a newspaper in the bottom of a chair as a bait for your models (cats love newspapers) and in a few moments your models will arrive to settle themselves comfortably to their satisfaction and yours far better than you could ever hope to arrange them.

For the next hour or two you can get innumerable sketches as they move about slightly in their sleep or change their positions. Newspapers make an excellent background as the cats silhouette against it.

In these pages the old friends' ovals and circles come to your aid and are well defined as you can see in the following sketches, one large oval for the outside area with smaller ones for the different parts.

In the picture above of the orange and the white cats there is a flowing line of forms melting into each other plus the spirit of rest.

Notice the strong beauty in the markings of the orange cat.

The single cat looking up for a brief moment calls for speedy work of the whole, with first work on the head as that would be first to change. You have a better chance for the body as that may remain the same from the shoulders back for several minutes.

The foreshortening of the heads and bodies of the white cats compel observation and thinking.

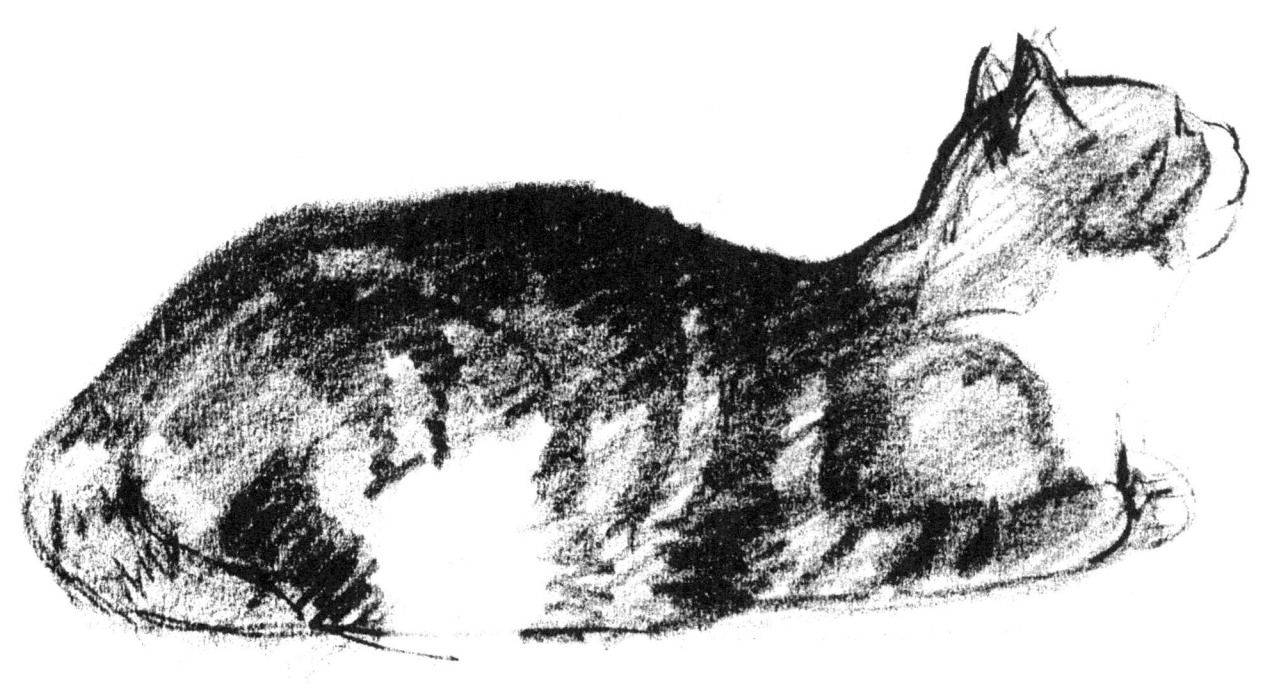

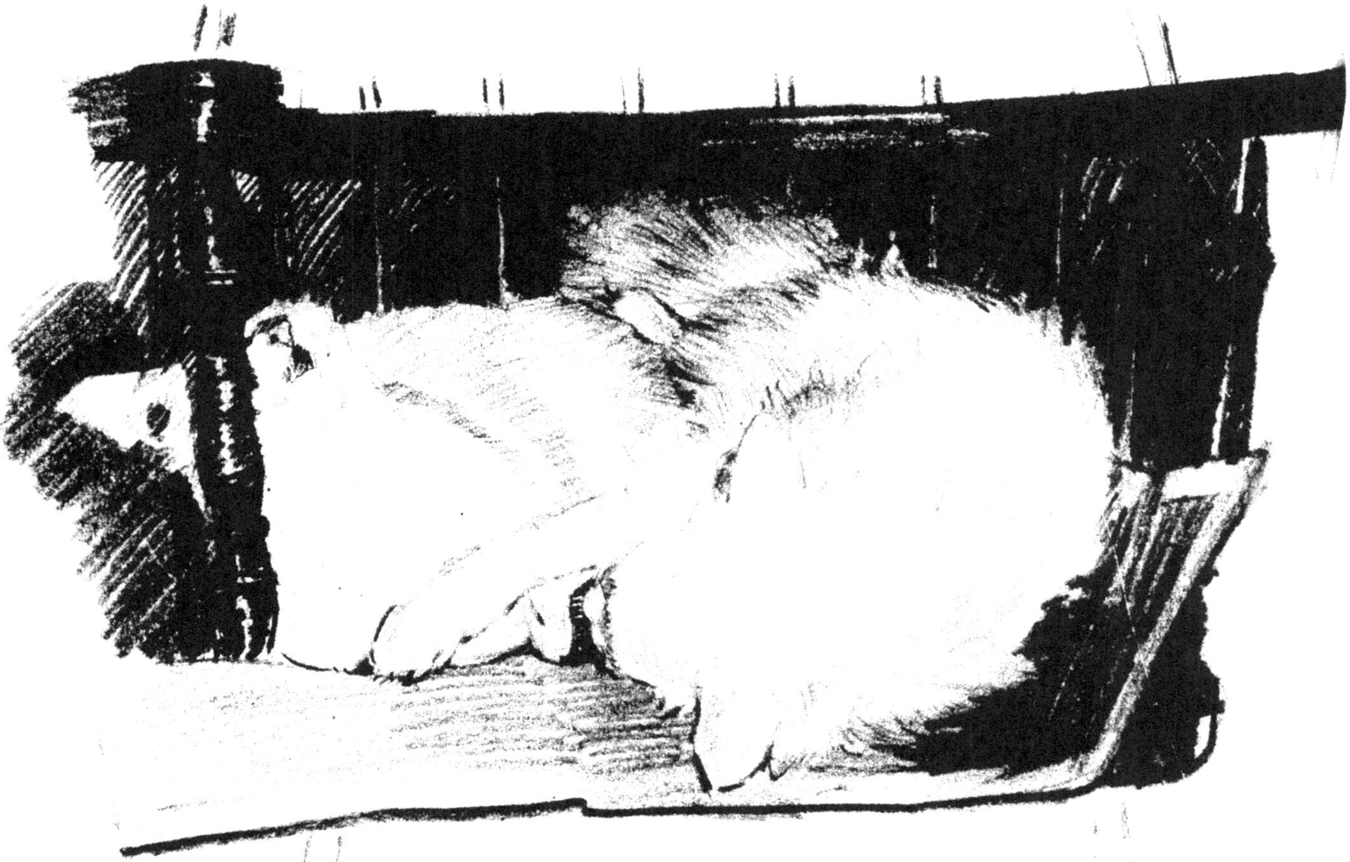

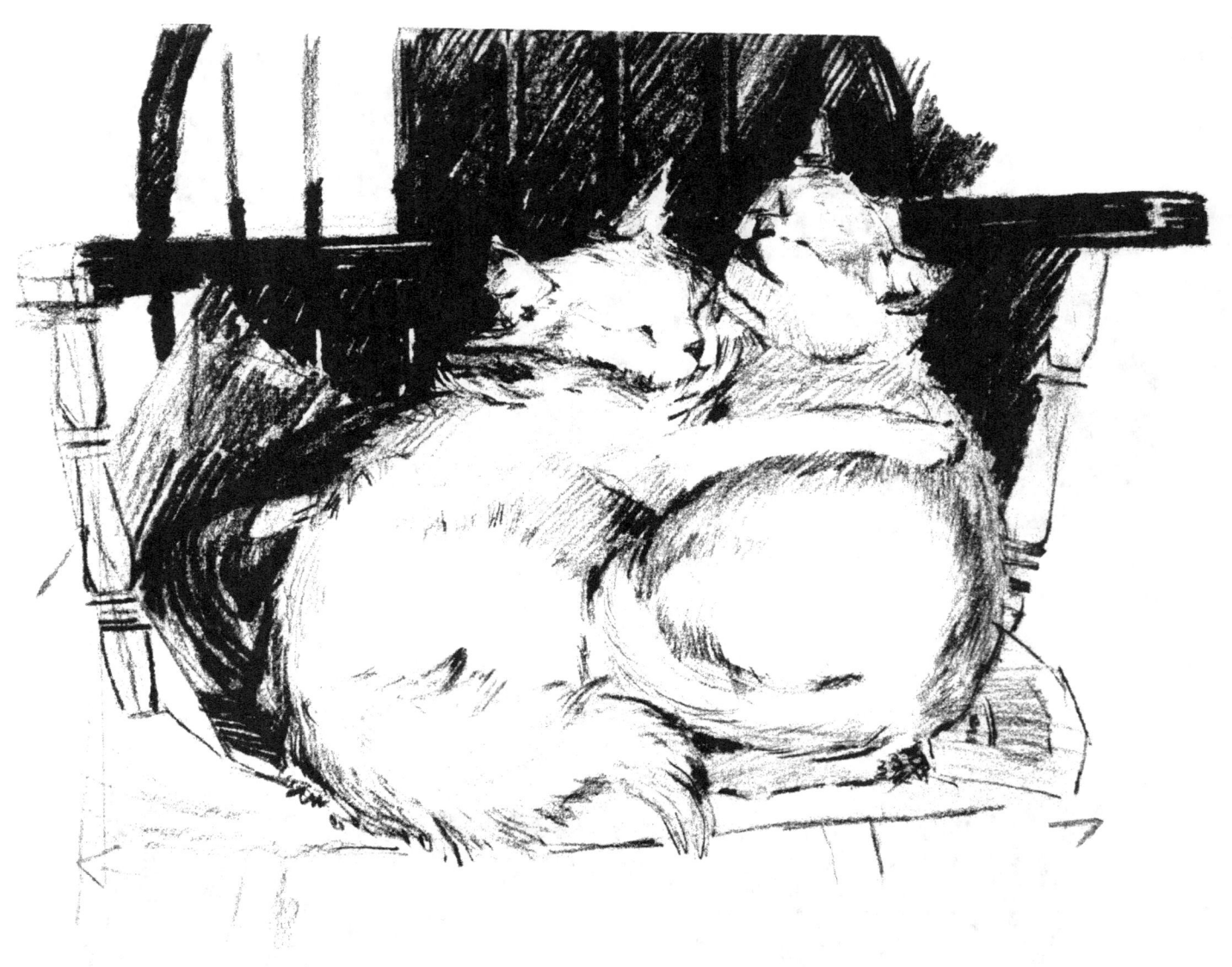

ATTITUDES

For us, the on-lookers, attitudes of the cat or two or more in a huddle are delightfully entertaining, whether they are snuggled together in sleep or awake.

The design of form and line is always present to lend enchantment to the picture and it is for you to snatch a record of it as fast as you can, for any moment you may lose the design you are working on. Do not despair, for it will be replaced by another design equally as beautiful.

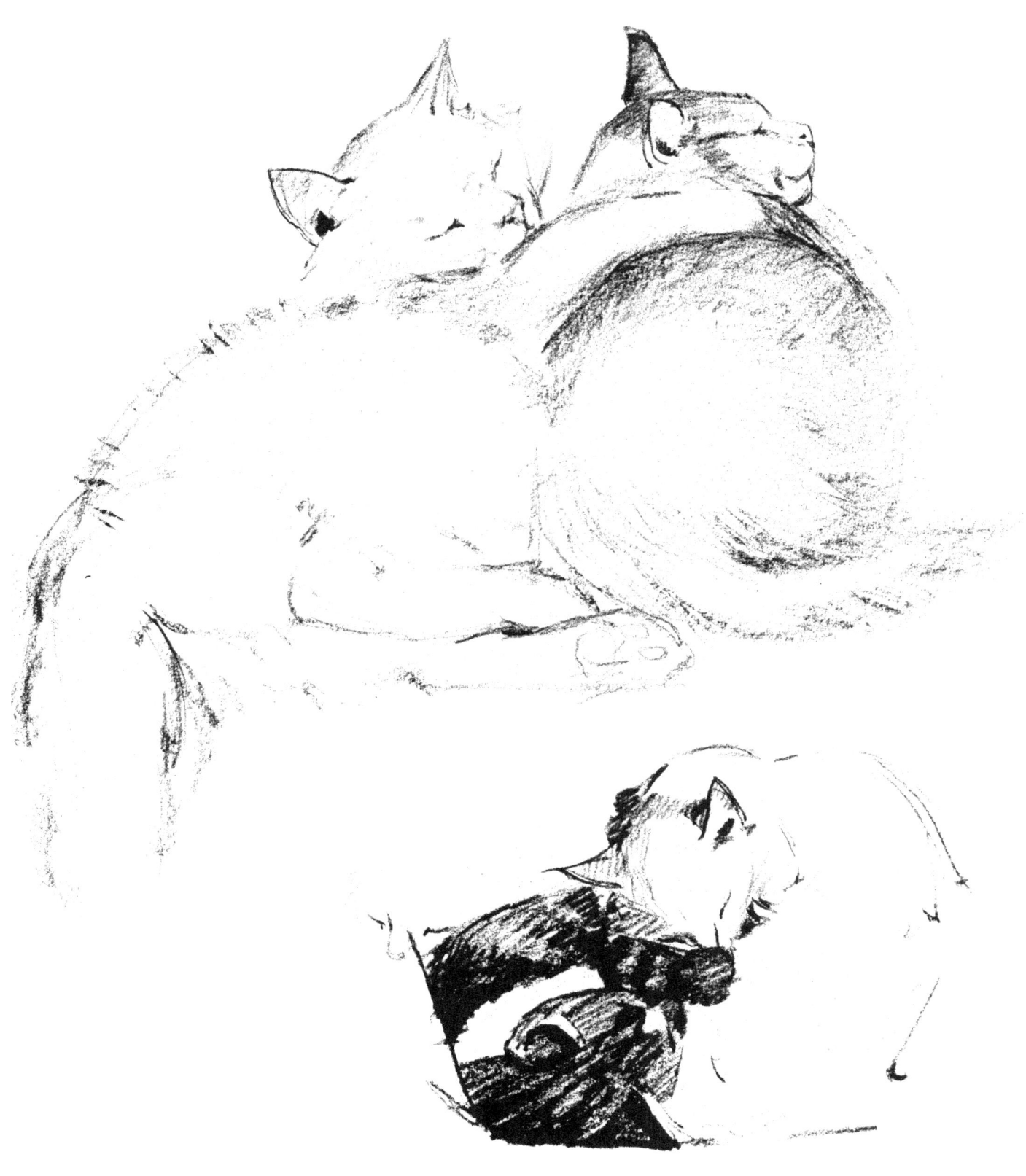

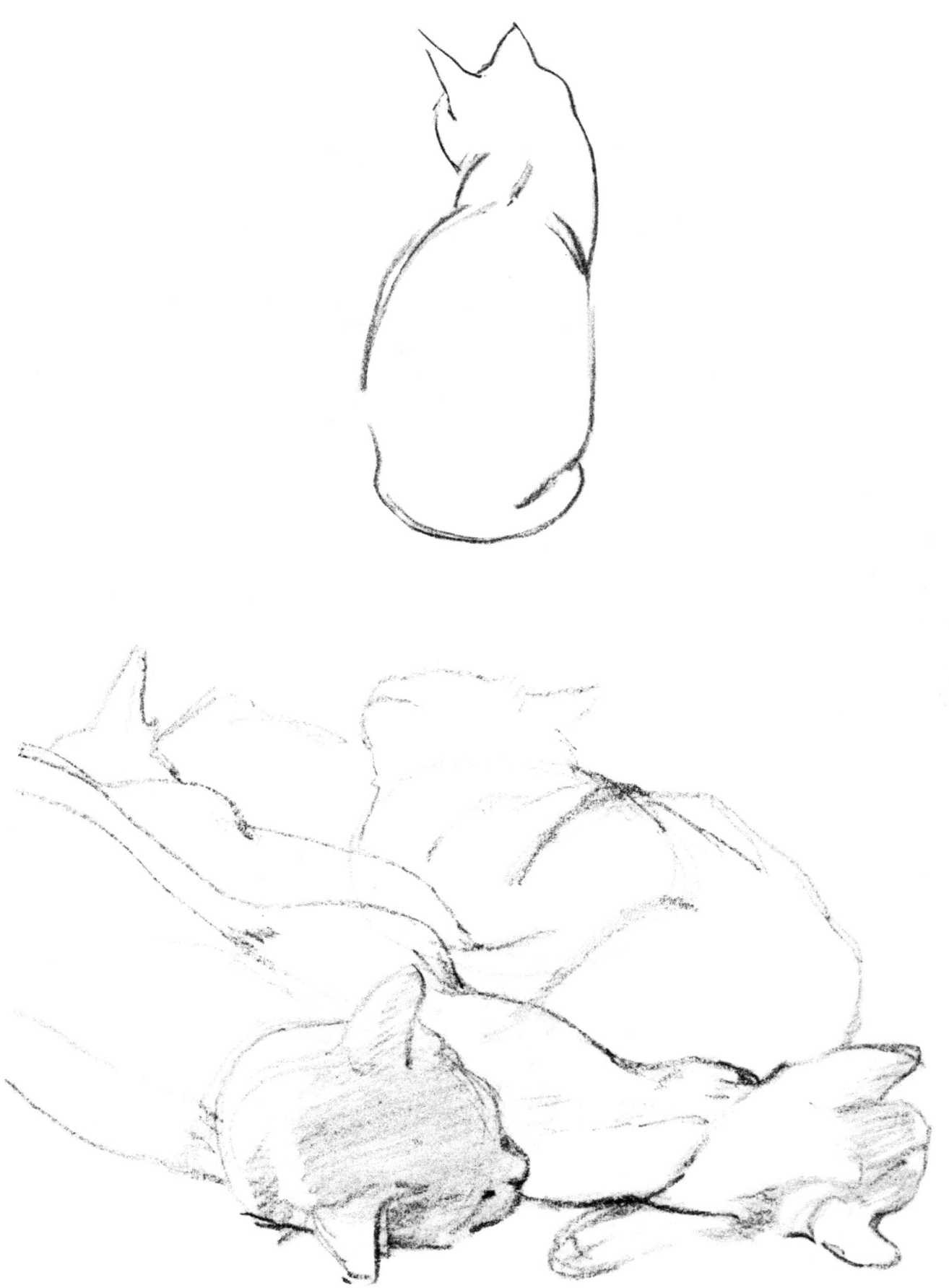

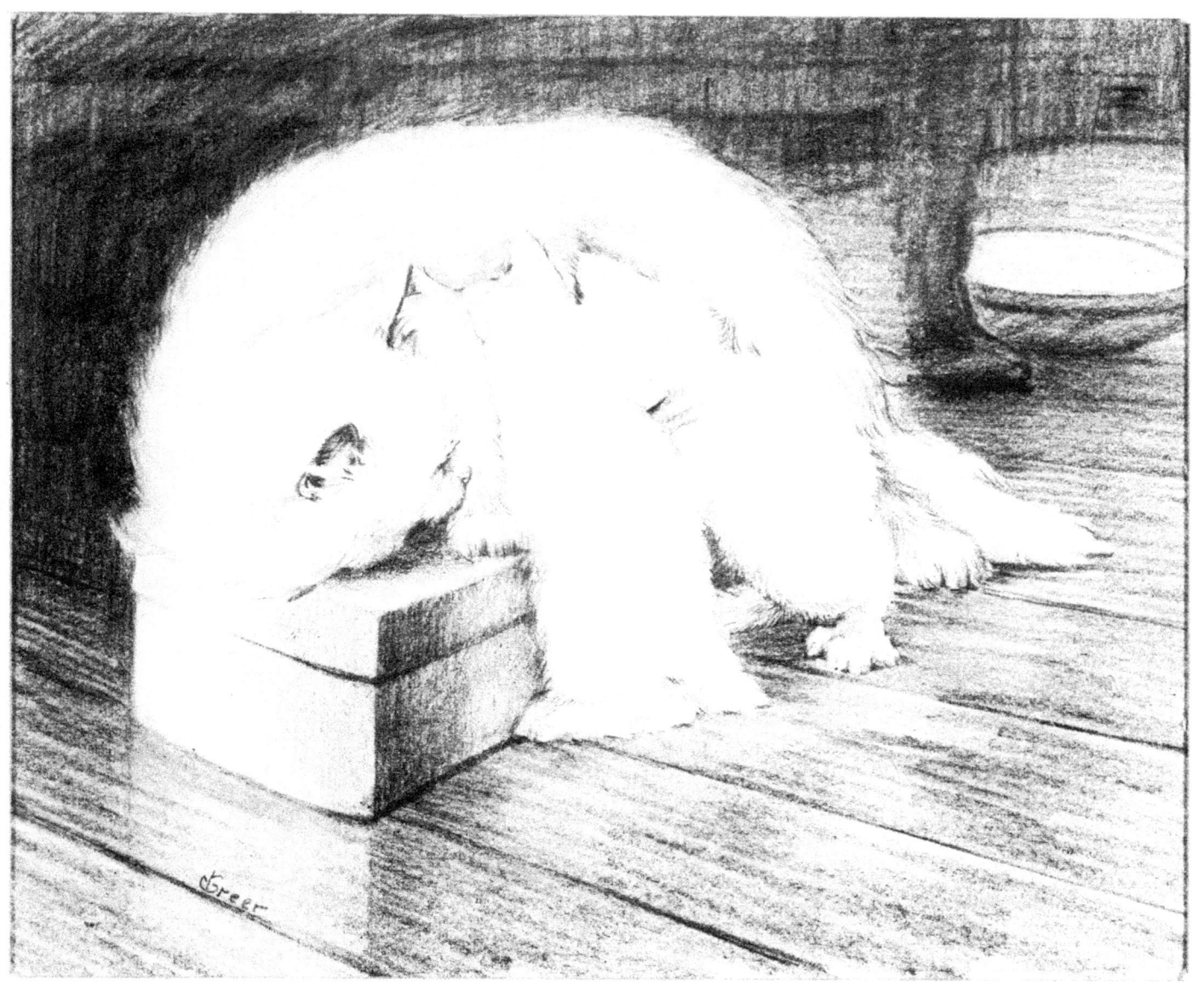

SUGGESTIONS

The energy and will to bring forth what you see will result in many hours of pleasure and time well spent, for to be able to draw one animal well will enable you to study and draw other species equally well.

You will find many "human interest" compositions among your sketches and a good caption helps greatly.

The name of the picture above is "The Milk Bar". It shows the patience of the mother cat and the born faith of the kittens that their mother provides and protects.

This sketch is a good example of a light mass against dark.

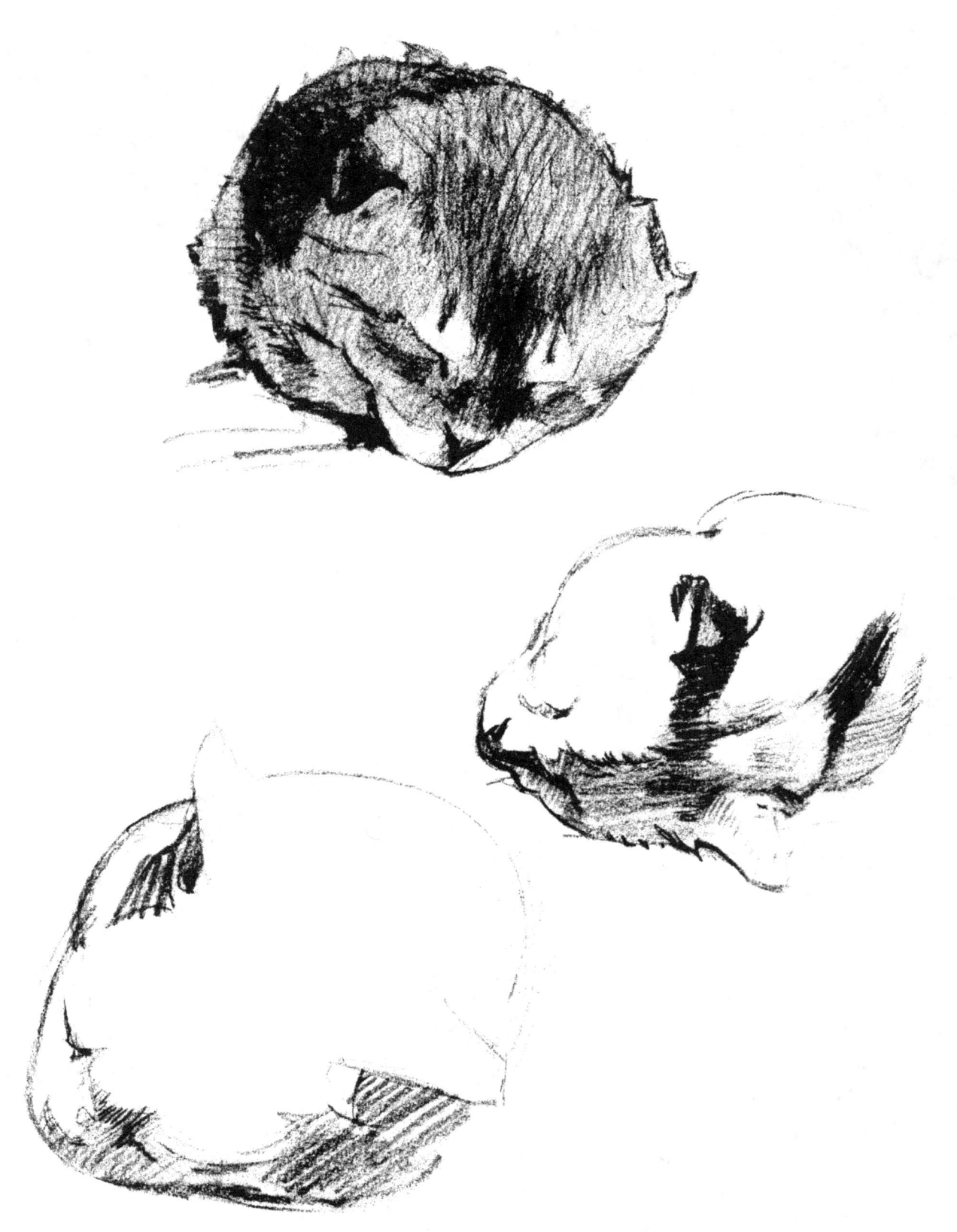

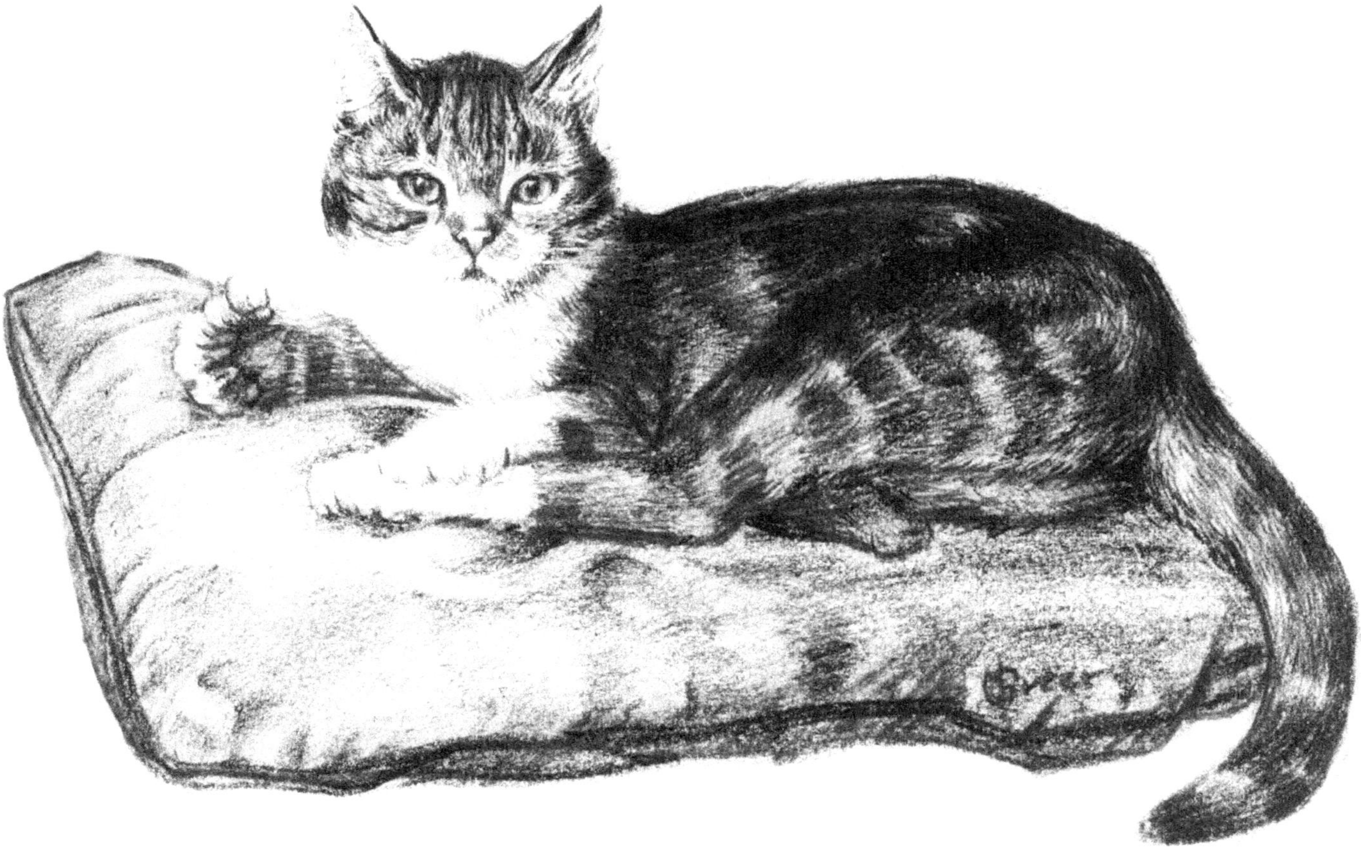

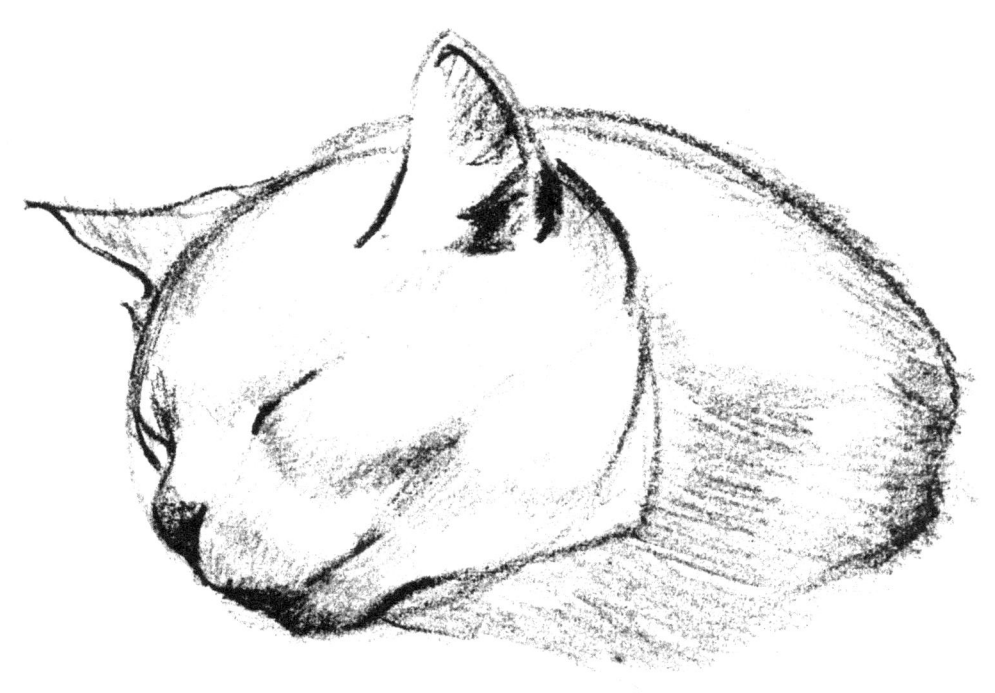

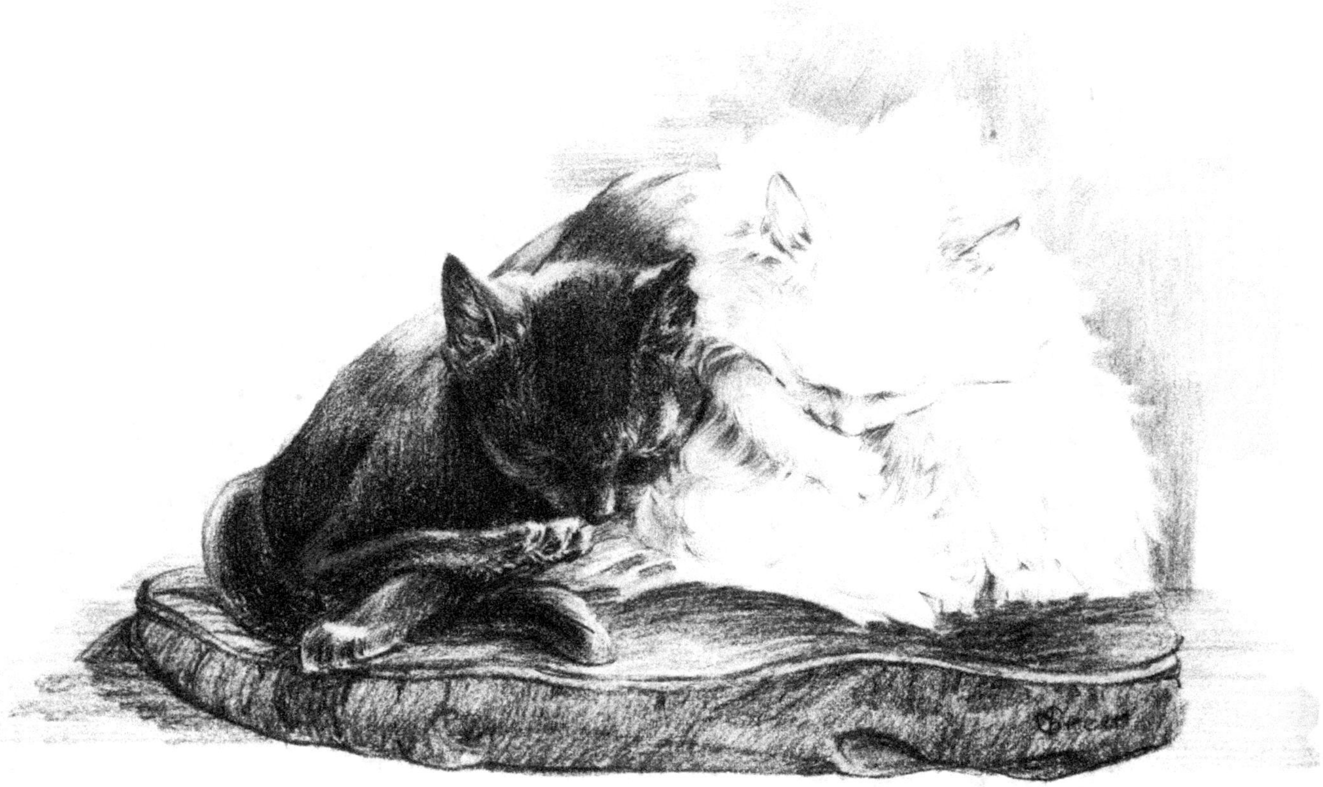

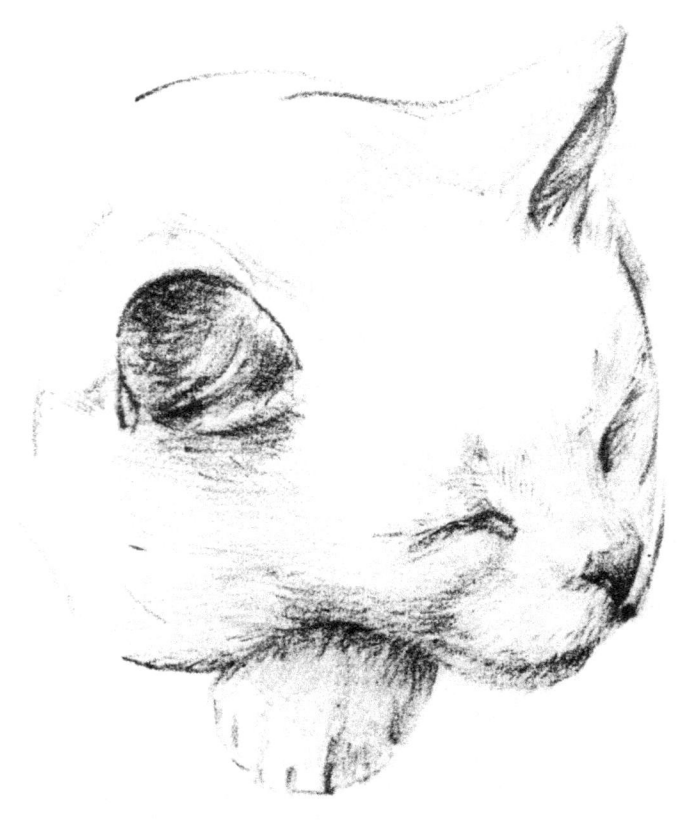

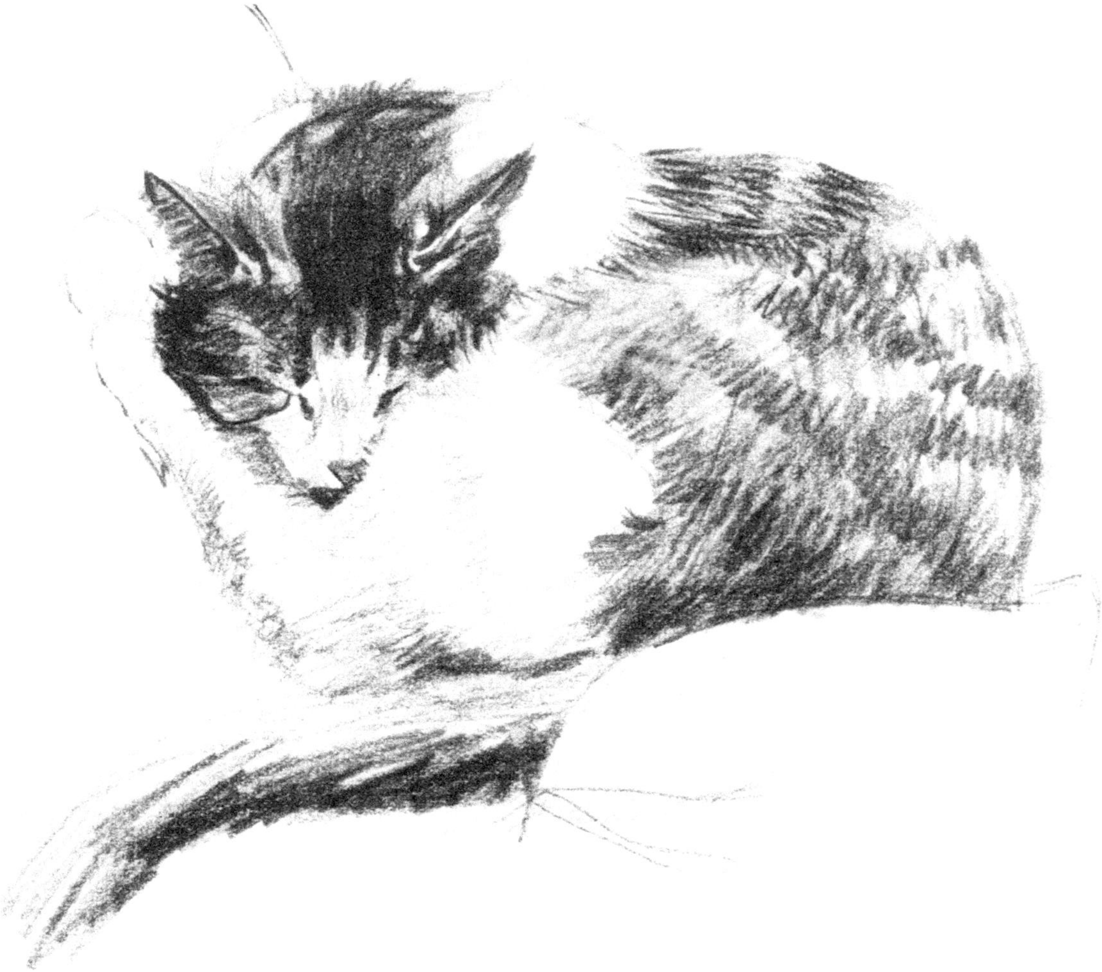

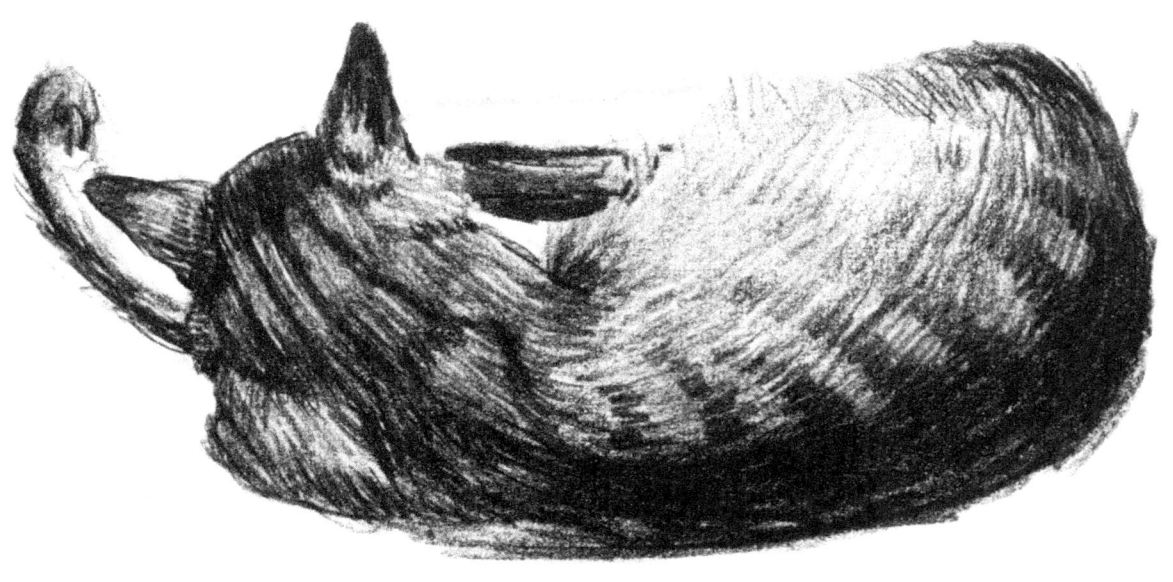

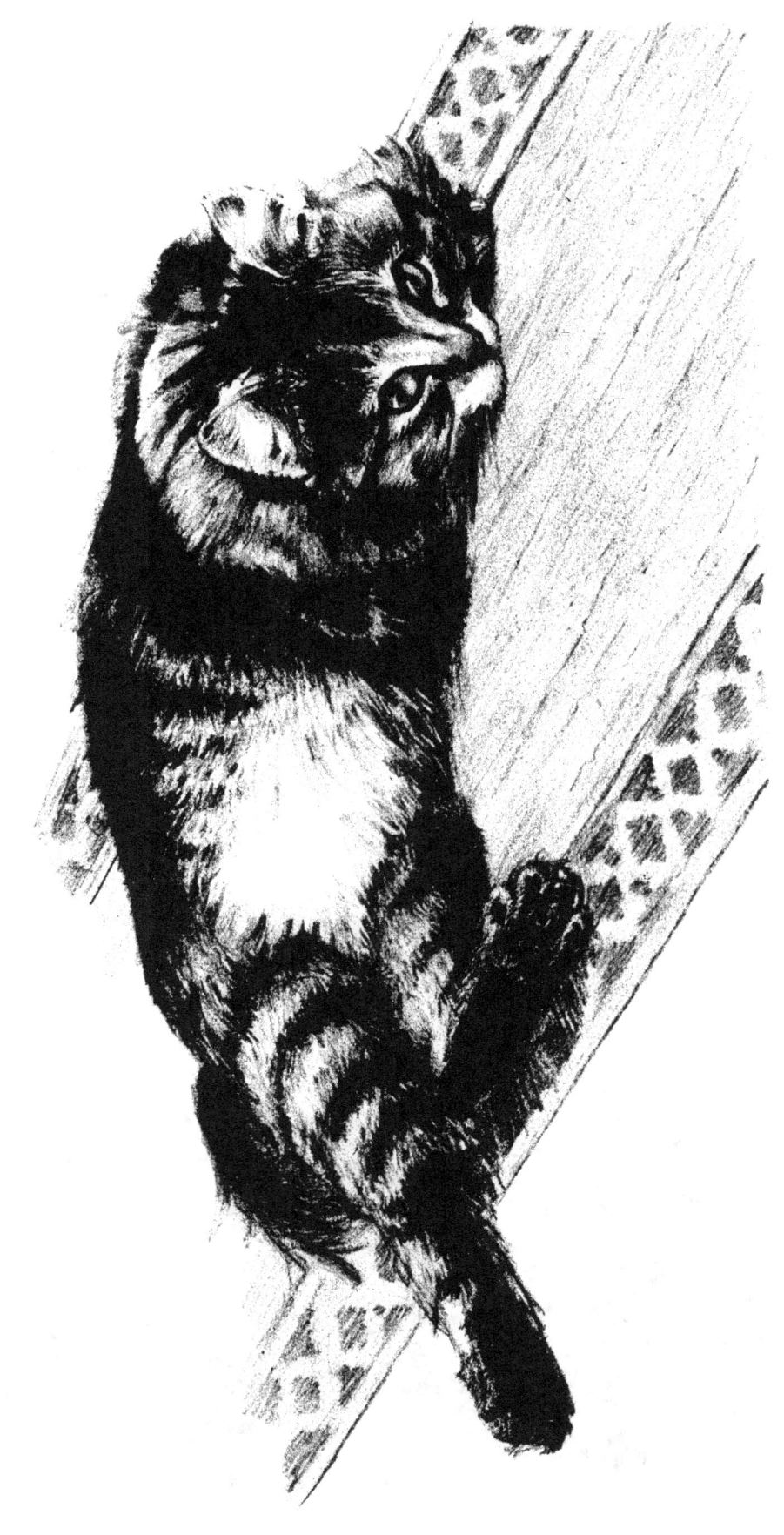

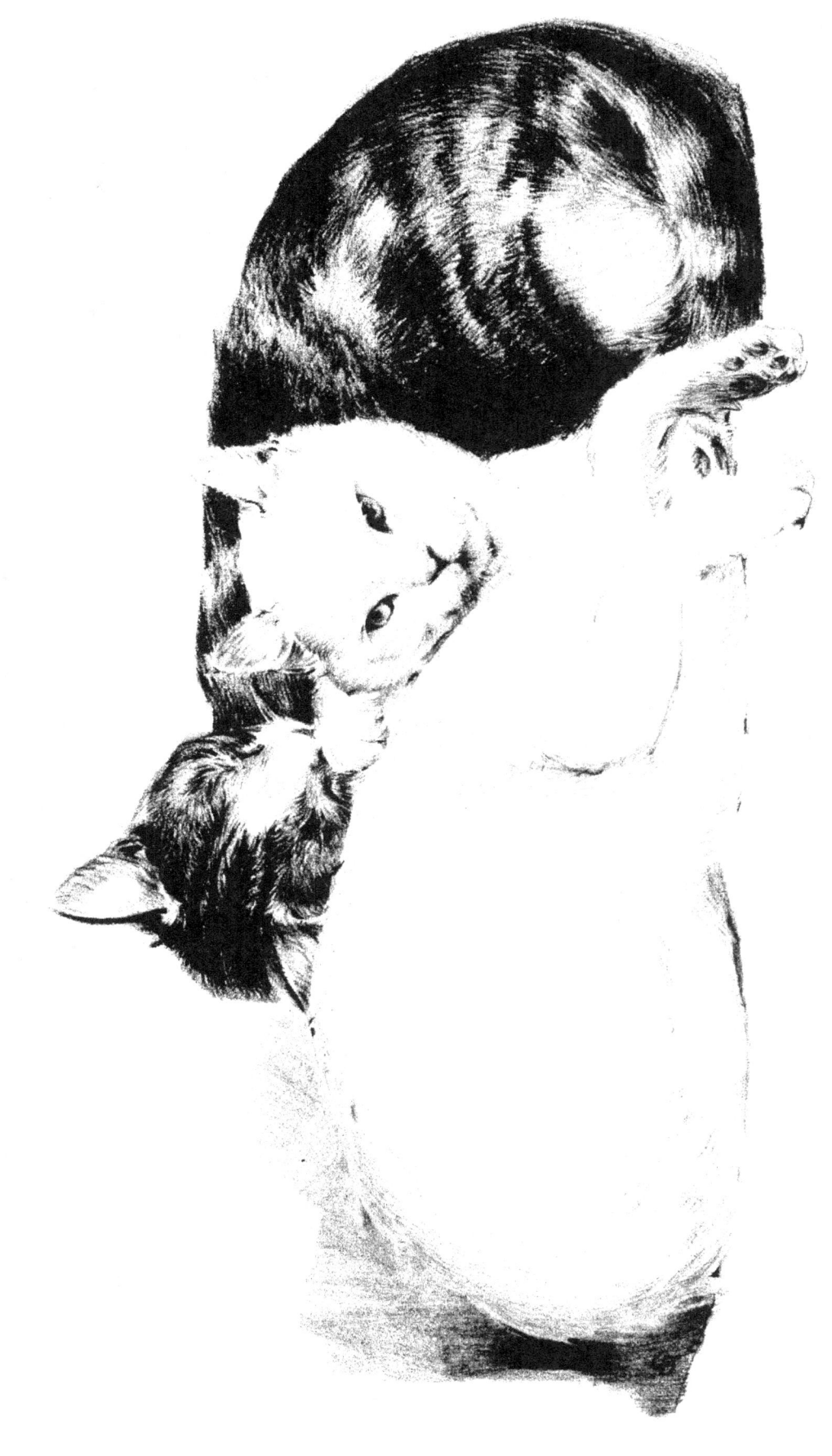

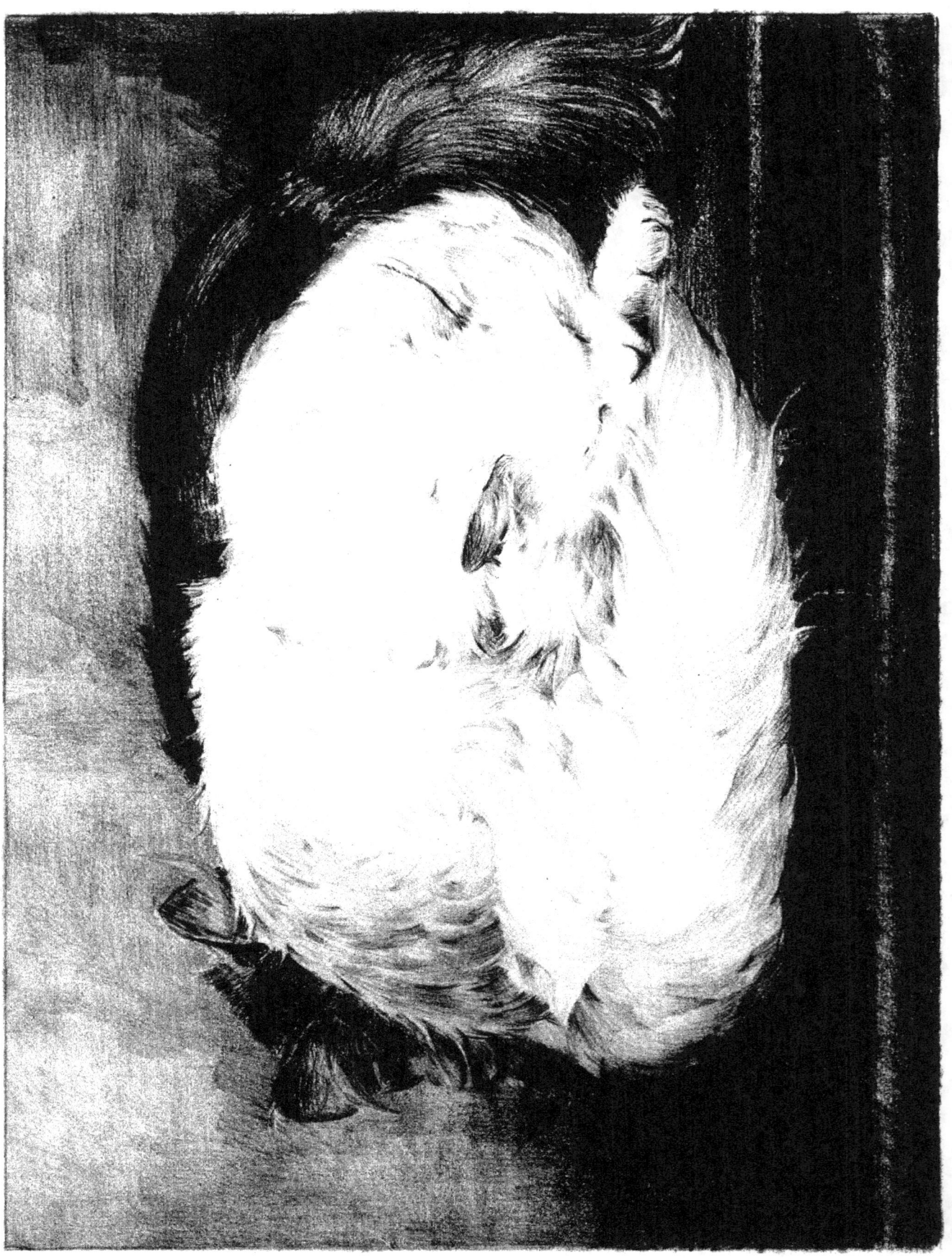

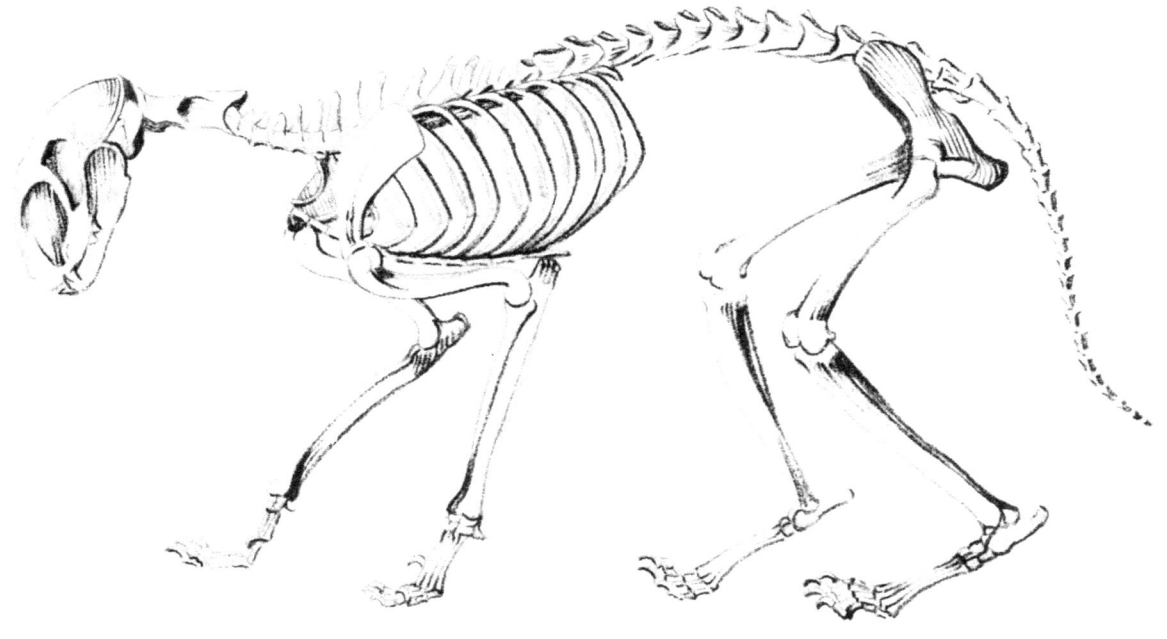

Coachwhip Publications

CoachwhipBooks.com

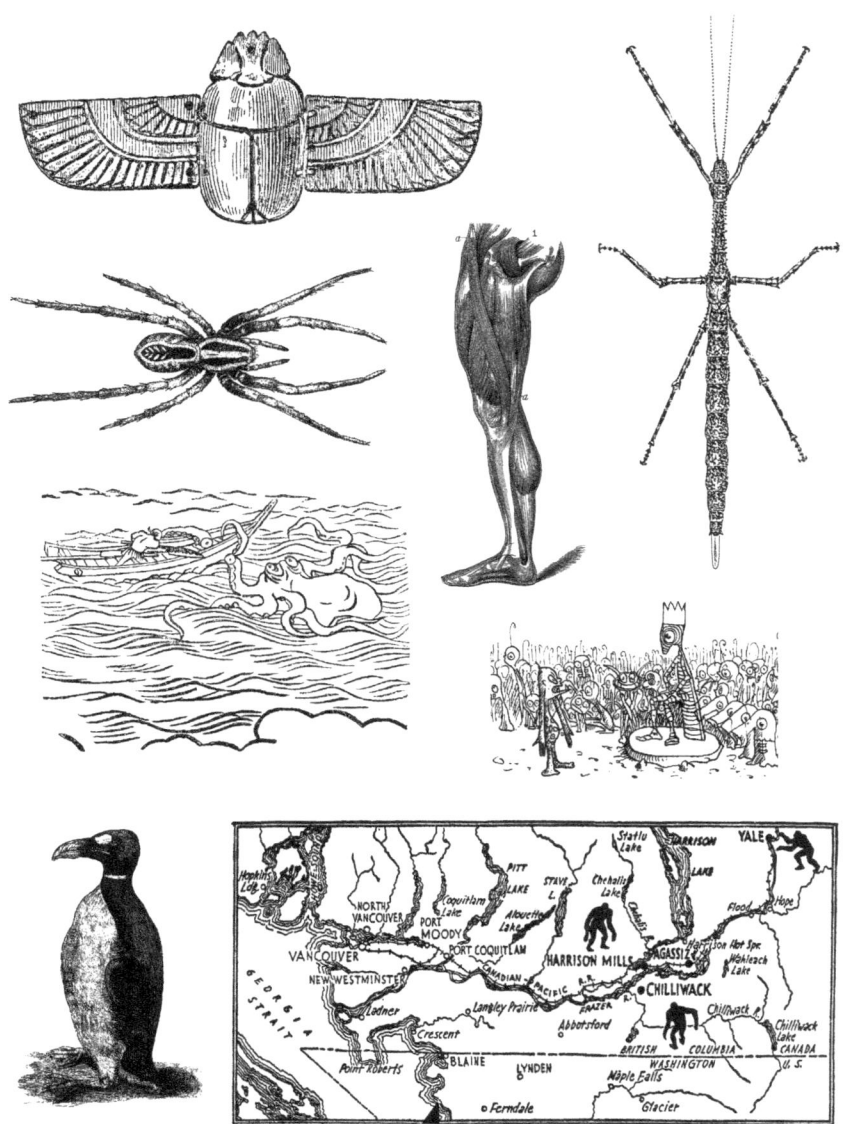

www.ingramcontent.com/pod-product-compliance
Lightning Source LLC
Chambersburg PA
CBHW081304170526
45165CB00011B/3408